NOT WITHOUT
THE HEAD

NOT WITHOUT
THE HEAD

AN INSIGHTFUL GUIDE FOR MEN TO EMBRACE GOD'S INSTRUCTIONS
FOR SUCCESS IN MARRIAGE, FAMILY, AND COMMUNITY

FREDRICK EZEJI-OKOYE

Carpenter's Son Publishing

Published by Carpenter's Son Publishing, Franklin, TN

Published in association with Larry Carpenter of Christian Book Services, LLC

Cover Design, Editing, and Interior Design by Adept Content Solutions

Printed in the United States of America

ISBN: 978-1-952025-42-6

FOREWORD

Grace Bwanhot and Debo Ijiwola

Debo Ijiwola
Co-Lead Pastor, The CityLight Church, Chicago

Today, Bro. Fred serves as a dedicated member of the usher team at our church, and yet leads a global ministry which includes the Men of Faith Network, a ministry that encourages men to thrive in the leadership of their homes, ministry, and society. I've been privileged to attend a few of the Men of Faith Network meetings. I feel tremendously blessed, seeing men from all walks of life under his leadership surrender their reputation, gather together as brethren around the word of God, love on each other, and pray for each other. It's always a beautiful sight, just as described in Psalm 133:1. It also speaks volumes about the heart of the leader, Bro. Fred.

Not without the Head is a much-needed response and a wake-up call to the crucial but missing foundation of godly leadership of fathers that has led to the moral decay in our society. We are deeply traumatized by the absence of godly fathers, whether it be fathers who are physically absent, spiritually absent, morally absent, relationally absent, or financially absent. It is also a call to action for men to rise up in their sonship and reflect the true nature of God that has been deposited within them without reserve.

For the earnest expectation of the creation eagerly waits for the revealing of the sons of God. (Rom. 8:19 NKJV)

The home is the foundational unit of our world at large, so leadership that will truly impact our communities, societies, and the world must begin in our homes. Bro. Fred, with a God-given passion for godly transformation in men, shares this timely message in a very unique writing style supported with personal stories that you can identify with. He and other men share their stories so vividly they grip your heart and move you to action.

The examples of vulnerability shared from his own personal struggles will not only cause you to self-reflect but give you hope that the same God who helped them can also help you if you're struggling and are willing to submit to His leadership. The principles shared in this book not only challenge men but equip men with practical tools in their submission to the leadership of Christ who is the head of every man. This book will also help women to learn how to support and pray for their husbands as they grow in their journey of leadership.

I encourage you to read with an open mind and study this book along with the scriptures shared. As you do your part, the Holy Spirit will shine the healing and transforming light of His word into the broken areas of your life and make you the leader that God has destined you to be!

***

Grace Bwanhot

When I met Brother Fred over ten years ago at an African Christian fellowship, he was a young, godly man full of passion for the things of the Lord, always hungry for more, especially anything that has to do with the husband/wife relationship. He asked questions about this subject, shared personal struggles, and a sincere desire to have a good marriage and family. He did not hide his frustrations either, as you will see after you read this book. But the beauty of it all is how God used every experience to get us to what we are about to experience as we journey with him through reading this simple but clear message from God, affirming your God-given privilege as men. There was a heart cry from within that kept wanting to understand this marriage institution to do it right. It was no surprise when we started a monthly couples Bible study, Bro. Fred was all in. Like many people, especially men who are always in a hurry, he was expecting a quick fix, but that was not the case. God had his hand on him and gave him sufficient grace and the right woman to slow him down.

Brother Fred shares here with a passion, not just rules and steps to being a successful head of the family, which are not bad in themselves, but so easy to be misused and abandoned. Rather, he shares a deep-hearted issue about walking with God according to His plan and enjoying a life of true freedom by leading your family through serving. His testimony, as well as that of others in this book, shows you that it is not an easy task—but it is doable by God's grace and your willingness and availability.

Bro. Fred acknowledges that most men carry wounds from their past, and some of you are currently being wounded even by the loved ones you are trying to protect. Remember, it is a battle worth fighting by relying on the grace of God and His sufficiency to carry you through. His heart's cry and plea to you is this, "Do not give up by letting the enemy have the final say."

***

CONTENTS

INTRODUCTION

I had all the energy you could think of while growing up. I considered my home a playground for me and my twin sister. My sister and I were last of seven siblings, the babies of the house. We considered nothing else as important as playtime, which was always a free, enjoyable time ,but there were also those moments that were so exceptional: "The Dad Presence!"

Dad's presence always made a difference. He disciplined us for littering the house, and checked on school homework and whether dishes or laundry were done. I grew up hating all his check-up actions with a passion. I never understood why in the world he denied us some of those fun times. For him, it was all about discipline and balancing life, but for Mom—you cannot take away the caring, nurturing, and encouragement. She was always there for us, especially in those emotional moments when we thought Dad was just being mean. Dad's decisions, I now know, were more factual, while Mom's were emotional with a soft touch.

Apart from academic lessons, Dad also introduced vocational training, including developing my skills in playing the piano. I disliked those decisions at the time because they collided with my fun time. Again, why in the world would I ever want to have a dad who limited my fun times? This attitude, or rather, this negative mind-set affected my concentration on learning to play the piano. I started having problems with the trainer and won at getting myself kicked out the class. Little did I know how negatively it would affect my future.

How did I get off that piano-lesson hook, you wonder? Well, I went straight to Mom and carefully narrated my story, convincing her that the teacher bullied me. No parent would tolerate that. Mom believed me, but Dad felt there must be something beyond my explanation. Again, his thoughts were more factual than emotional. So, he put an investigation hat on and concluded that all I had said was nothing but a flimsy excuse to avoid training. My response was to cry to Mom and emphatically tell her I wanted no more classes and that I would rather concentrate on academic lessons (which, thinking about it now, I didn't do either) other than vocational lessons.

My mom's heart was won over, and she pleaded on my behalf. Dad, being a man filled with wisdom, let go. It so excited me that I won, but years down the line, I realized it was the dumbest decision I ever made in life. To this day, I still pay the consequences for the path I chose. I attended a Christian high school where they gave the students who could play the piano preferential treatment by exempting them from all physical work time, such as scrubbing and cleaning the dormitory and its surroundings. Instead, those times were changed to allow them piano practice time. It hit me hard that I could have been one of those privileged students. To date, every time I'm looking for an organist to play the piano for the men's fellowship days that I organize, I'm reminded of Dad's vision for me back then (introducing a vocational lesson), which I failed to achieve.

I tried to drop out of high school, but Dad would not let me. As usual, I went to Mom with my million reasons and excuses on why I should. This time around, Dad stood his ground and clarified that whatever my vision was, it was very necessary to have a basic education before engaging or pursuing those dreams. Because he refused to relent, I graduated from high school and, on my own, graduated from the university. Looking back, I thank God for the educational qualifications I possess—all due to a dad who put his foot down to ensure I finished high school and continued to a university. I cannot thank him enough. With age and reflection, I always thank God, whose grace allowed me to grow up under the supervision of a responsible and involved dad.

I had other rough times like every other youth and teenager faces today, but my dad was always on my back. His presence made an immense difference in my decisions. Maybe because of my mom's caring nature and emotional decision-making, I never quivered at her presence or reactions at home, but it was different with Dad. I always feared his presence and reactions, which had a positive effect on me.

After I graduated from the university, many within my sphere of friends and associates were into fraudulent businesses and making fast money. I was tempted daily to join but did not dare dabble in it because I anticipated Dad's reaction. I could not figure out nor come up with a reasonable explanation I could give him if I were to dubiously start making such quick money. I shied away from those businesses because I had a dad who would investigate me and possibly turn me over to the authorities if need be. That positive influence my dad had on me served as a checkmate over my juvenile delinquencies before my Creator (our Lord, Jesus Christ), arrested my soul, and to date, I have not regretted surrendering my life to Jesus. To the glory of God, my parents are proud today, especially my dad.

This same wheel I must say, is going around now as my wife and I transition into parenting. We have three kids, ages thirteen, eight, and seven. It is very ironic that my childhood feelings toward my dad are the same way my oldest son feels about me now. I always encourage him, telling him that he will grow up and realize how important all that I do at home is. I always share my story with him and stay very close to him, so he won't have any regrets in life. I have regretted all those disciplinary cautions I kicked against and, to this day, I still hear my dad's voice echoing in my ears. Dad used to tell me back then that in the future I would realize how important his actions were. He only meant to help and mold me. I am paying heavily for his decisions that I kicked against. Those that I followed have helped shape me to who I am today. One thing for sure is that I cannot change the past, but I can change the future. I have made a conscious and intentional decision to stay involved with my kids and never give up on working toward seeing a better me in them.

An important question arising from my childhood experiences is "Are men more factual than emotional?" My answer is yes to men being factual. I believe that men and women are wired differently. Men are more factual and more disciplinary than women. This brings into focus the purpose of my writing this book.

This book is not to undermine the creative power of women in our society. I encourage men to stand up and take their responsibilities at home seriously to reduce the burden of single parenthood, which is borne mostly by women. Families without fathers present in the household are the cause of great harm in our society. Please consider the following information and statistics that triggered the passion for writing this book:

Father-Absent Homes: Implications for Criminal Justice and Mental Health Professionals
Jerrod Brown, MA, MS, MS, MS
https://www.mnpsych.org/index.php%3Foption%3Dcom_dailyplanetblog%26view%3Dentry%26category%3Dindustry%2520news%26id%3D54
The number of children who grow up without a father in the home in the United States has reached concerning levels. There exists a considerable research base that suggests that children raised in households lacking a father experience psychosocial problems with greater frequency than children with a father in the home (Allen & Daly, 2007). These problems have been found to extend into adolescence and adulthood and include an increased risk of substance use, depression, suicide, poor school performance, and contact with the criminal justice system (Allen & Daly, 2007). Lack of paternal involvement has also been associated with a higher likelihood of being bullied and experiencing abuse (Allen & Daly, 2007). Educating uninvolved fathers and helping them play a more active role in their child's life could benefit both families and communities. To bring this into focus, the present article aims to highlight ten adverse outcomes that may result from the absence of a father in a child's life: (1) Perceived abandonment; (2) attachment issues; (3) child abuse; (4) childhood obesity; (5) criminal justice involvement; (6) gang involvement; (7) mental health issues; (8) poor school performance; (9) poverty and homelessness; and (10) substance use.

Please note that the above-mentioned statistics focus only on the absence of fathers for the purpose of this book. I am very aware of the negative impact of mother-absence in homes and its implications for criminal justice and mental health.

Associations between Father Absence and Age of First Sexual Intercourse

https://www.ncbi.nlm.nih.gov/pmc/articles/PMC2939716/

As the rate of sexually active American teenagers has increased dramatically across the second half of the twentieth century (Kotchik, Shaffer, Forehand, & Miller, 2001), there has been a corresponding surge in investigations of teenage sexuality. Research consistently identifies the family structure as one salient antecedent of earlier sexual activity in teenagers. Compared to children raised by both biological parents, children who are raised in households without their biological father present exhibit both an earlier age of first intercourse and significantly increased rates of teenage pregnancy (Ellis et al., 2003; Hogan & Kitagawa, 1985; Kiernan & Hobcraft, 1997; Newcomer & Udry, 1987; Quinlan, 2003; Wight, Williamson, & Henderson, 2006).

Several explanatory mechanisms have been proposed for this important association, all of which implicate the environmental effects of father absence. Interpreting broad epidemiological associations between family structure and teenage sexuality can be problematic, however, because children reared in father-absent families differ from those raised in father-present households in a myriad of ways that potentially impact both family structure and sexual behavior. Therefore, the observed association could be attributable to the non-random selection of individuals predisposed for early sexual activity into father-absent families, rather than proximal environmental influences.

It's very obvious that the absence of fathers, if not addressed consistently, the issue of teenage pregnancy will keep on increasing .

Not without the Head

> *So God created mankind in his own image, in the image of God he created them; male and female he created them.* (Gen. 1:27)

There is a male and female factor created in God's image, which is in existence in the spiritual realm (Heaven). But then, there is a garden God planted in the East in Eden called the Garden of Eden. This represents the physical realm (Earth). Our creator is a God of orderliness; He desired that mankind manage the physical realm, so He first formed man to do the work. The man became the head, which can also be known as the manager. He was given instructions on how to manage, and thereafter, God said it is not good for the man to be alone. He considered the volume of work that the man is doing and said the man would need a helper who could be considered as a co-manager to govern. He tested the intelligence of the man by bringing him other creations. The man named them but found no companion until finally, God created the female factor from out of the rib of the man. The man felt relieved and named the female *woman*, meaning my co-laborer.

> OUR CREATOR IS A GOD OF ORDERLINESS; HE DESIRED THAT MANKIND MANAGE THE PHYSICAL REALM SO HE FIRST FORMED MAN TO DO THE WORK. THE MAN BECAME THE HEAD, WHICH CAN ALSO BE KNOWN AS THE MANAGER.

> Now no shrub had yet appeared on the earth and no plant had yet sprung up, for the LORD God had not sent rain on the earth and there was no one to work the ground, but streams came up from the earth and watered the whole surface of the ground. Then the LORD God formed a man from the dust of the ground and breathed into his nostrils the breath of life, and the man became a living being. Now the LORD God had planted a garden in the

east, in Eden; and there he put the man he had formed. The Lord God made all kinds of trees grow out of the ground—trees that were pleasing to the eye and good for food. In the middle of the garden was the tree of life and the tree of the knowledge of good and evil. A river watering the garden flowed from Eden; from there it was separated into four headwaters. The name of the first is the Pishon; it winds through the entire land of Havilah, where there is gold. (The gold of that land is good; aromatic resin and onyx are also there.) The name of the second river is the Gihon; it winds through the entire land of Cush. The name of the third river is the Tigris; it runs along the east side of Ashur. And the fourth river is the Euphrates. The Lord God took the man and put him in the Garden of Eden to work it and take care of it. And the Lord God commanded the man, "You are free to eat from any tree in the garden; but you must not eat from the tree of the knowledge of good and evil, for when you eat from it you will certainly die." The Lord God said, "It is not good for the man to be alone. I will make a helper suitable for him." Now the Lord God had formed out of the ground all the wild animals and all the birds in the sky. He brought them to the man to see what he would name them; and whatever the man called each living creature, that was its name. So the man gave names to all the livestock, the birds in the sky and all the wild animals. But for Adam, no suitable helper was found. So the Lord God caused the man to fall into a deep sleep; and while he was sleeping, he took one of the man's ribs and then closed up the place with flesh. Then the Lord God made a woman from the rib he had taken out of the man, and he brought her to the man. The man said, "This is now bone of my bones and flesh of my flesh; she shall be called 'woman,' for she was taken out of man." That is why a man leaves his father and mother and is united to his wife, and they become one flesh. (Gen. 2:5–24)

Note that before the woman, God formed man first, placed him in the garden to work, and gave him instructions before the arrival of the woman. Every man needs to understand that we have work to do before getting married to a woman. We ought to understand that the instruction on how to lead is the work of man because he is the head. This will be discussed much later in this book. Men are the visionaries of their home, considered to be the head, and women are to help the men fulfill that vision. Unfortunately, we experience the opposite of this principle these days, which has led to too many divorces and so many kids growing up without a father figure. When God decided to create man first, it was not an error. God created everything, and everything he created was good. That is why the man leaves his parents and enters his own Garden of Eden (family) with his wife in unity. The Bible never mentioned that the woman leaves the parents, only the man.

> EVERY MAN NEEDS TO UNDERSTAND THAT WE HAVE WORK TO DO BEFORE GETTING MARRIED TO A WOMAN.

That is why a man leaves his father and mother and is united to his wife, and they become one flesh. (Gen. 2:24)

At wedding ceremonies, this is symbolized with the bride's father handing over his daughter to another man at the altar. The message of this is to handle with care; she is your helper—unite with her and manage the garden collectively. The woman now drops her maiden name and adopts the man's name for life. The man proposes to a woman and not the woman to the man (though we sometimes see the reverse these days). But remember, the man must have been working with instructions (vision) before proceeding to have a helper. This makes the man the head. So, with God's principle of the creation of mankind, it is highly unlikely to have a fulfilled family without the head. Man, not being at the head, is a malfunctioning of God's designed agenda.

Paul also addressed it clearly that the man is the head of the wife, as Christ is the head of the church. Therefore, every man should have Jesus Christ as their role model. The church today is not perfect and can never be perfect, but Jesus loves the church unconditionally. Let this be the mind-set of every man. Men's responsibilities require giving unconditional love to be able to accomplish the role of being the head in the family.

For the husband is the head of the wife as Christ is the head of the church, his body, of which he is the Savior. (Eph. 5:23)

I love this quote: "The man may be the head of the household. But the woman is the neck, and she can turn the head whichever way she pleases" (Nia Vardalos). This popular quote confirms that being the head has not and should not make a man a dictator. It is a privilege and

PAUL ALSO ADDRESSED IT CLEARLY THAT THE MAN IS THE HEAD OF THE WIFE, AS CHRIST IS THE HEAD OF THE CHURCH. THEREFORE, EVERY MAN SHOULD HAVE JESUS CHRIST AS THEIR ROLE MODEL.

should be handled wisely. Whether the head or the neck per se, the most important is that the man has a helper to manage the garden (family) collectively. Being the head requires a lot, and that is exactly what this book will help us discover.

CHAPTER ONE

BONDING

Do two walk together unless they have agreed to do so?
—Amos 3:3

Writing this book has not made me a specialist but has created a passion in me to stir up men to make their leadership role important at home. We are all works in progress with diverse weaknesses here and there, but the greatest task or challenge is sticking with one wedded wife till death do us part.

After every honeymoon, the reality of marriage comes into existence without a pre-notice. This is the period all promises made to one another during courtship is tested. I do not know about yours, but for me it was, "How do I get off?" Each time I was tempted to back off the marriage, the word of the Lord kept sounding very clear to me—the Lord hates divorce.

For the Lord God of Israel says that He hates divorce, for it covers one's garment with violence," says the Lord of hosts. Therefore take heed to your spirit, that you do not deal treacherously. (Mal. 2:16)

Each time I set my eyes on this verse of the scripture, I could not help but wonder if there is any way it could be rewritten or erased so I can find freedom. Thank God I am privileged to have the spiritual eyes to see and understand that when it comes to the word of God—what is written is written. There is no revised edition, and there can never be. And, thank God, by His grace I was not disobedient to the word of God because I could have added to the statistics of absent fathers.

Background

I am the last child in my family, although I have a twin. My wife is the firstborn child in her family. I grew up being pampered by parents and receiving gifts and cash from older siblings. For my wife, the reverse was the case. She has a giving nature. This became a huge problem for both of us. I could not understand why her actions and thoughts were all around how to help her siblings, while mine were on how I can still receive help from my siblings. This battle kept going on and on until one day, I gave up the fight and had to yield. Since I did, I found and have had peace.

I grew up with four sisters. I never did any kind of household or domestic chores like washing dishes or cleaning, and no cooking of any kind. One of my sisters is very gifted at cooking and an exhibition of her cooking skills nurtured the picture in my mind of how my family will look like. I spent most of my vacation at her matrimonial home and as a working wife and mum, she dedicated every Saturday of the month to cooking assorted varieties of food. I was part of her routine as I would normally drive her to the grocery stores where she bought everything in bulk. As soon as she arrived home, cooking commenced. I was there, more or less, to taste the food for her on such days. A home-cooked meal was never an issue at her home. So, while I was staying at her home, I imagined how my own home would look some-day and painted the picture that my wife would do the same. Little did I know that life is not always as we desire.

God knows the best and gives us compatible wives. God gave me mine, but my dream never came to pass. That sister of mine was the ideal wife-model picture I had, but my wife is the opposite. This became a big issue as I tried to change my wife to my pictured wife model, but the more I tried, the worse it became. Now, where do I run to? I used to hear the slogan that "marriage is not meant for the boys but the men." It dawned on me that I must manage the position, but with wisdom. The only option I had was to start learning about and helping with domestic chores like cooking. There is no greater teacher than getting into action. I started cooking, and by His grace, I got better at it. I never took a class, but the memory of hanging around my sister was God's divine intervention. God knows the future and allowed me time around my sister during those years. That experience registered. It was a seed, but I never knew my cooking potential until I left home. I now enjoy cooking for the family more than my wife does. My wife is a great cook but just does not enjoy cooking. She will rather embark on a period of fasting than cook.

Meanwhile, I kept focusing on my wife's weaknesses without realizing her strength. For me, as a man, I am very horrible when it comes to being handy at home. My wife is the handy person in our home. Can you imagine? This woman has never complained about this horrible weakness I have. Funny enough, her brothers are handy. I will never forget the very day the electricity went off in the entire house, right in the middle of the night. I was there, the head of the family but hadn't the faintest idea of what to do to fix it. While still thinking, my wife simply went downstairs to the basement and in a few minutes, all the lights in the house came back on. I cannot tell what she did or how she did it and to date, she remains the handy person in our home.

Within the space of our five years of experience in marriage, both of us are now able to bear and accommodate each other in areas of strengths and weaknesses. I carry out the journey faithfully because I now understand the meaning of *headship* at home. Does that mean that I am getting it right all the time? The answer is capital "NO." When I fall, I rise again—the primary objective for every man is to exercise patience during bonding.

> WHEN I FALL, I RISE AGAIN—THE PRIMARY OBJECTIVE FOR EVERY MAN IS TO EXERCISE PATIENCE DURING BONDING.

As I mentioned, nothing takes God unaware. He never makes an error and is a master planner. Always believe that whatever is happening is for a purpose. When I look back now, I always have a reason to thank God that my wife never succumbed to my pressure on her to cook as often and as much as I had wanted her to. Most of the food I was craving for or cooked back then is no longer the food I eat today. As of today, I eat less and do not even eat those types of food I had desired back then. So, cooking for me today has reduced drastically. I stopped eating those foods because of health reasons. Read in between the lines—I am still at it today, no longer eating the very type of foods that I was demanding back then at the early stages of our marriage with all the strength in me. Seriously, this very challenge on food was the area that made me consider quitting my marriage. Suppose I did get the divorce, I bet I would be regretting it this day. It will surprise you that many who go through a divorce do regret it much later in life (except under some exceptional circumstances, which are acceptable). This food issue that challenged my marriage and could have pushed me into a divorce is the same thing I shy away from these days, and this same type of food, I now know, could have sent me to my early grave.

Personality

My wife is an introvert while I am considered an extrovert. Blending these two can be very frustrating if you do not apply wisdom. I may not be able to prove this with statistics, but I feel that the reason most men who get sent early to their graves is due to their attempts to change their wives to become who they want them to become. My wife has never raised her voice at me regarding any issue, but she subtly fights her battles. I would rather have her yell at me. I remember my grumbles back in the day, mumbling why on earth I had to go grocery shopping and buy the food items, yet she would not do the cooking. I would yell and yell, and she would say nothing. I recall one of those days of my throwing tantrums about her usual no cooking; I found leftover food in the fridge. Luckily, there was still something to eat. But the next day, I came back from work, expecting to find well-prepared and garnished food since I had poured out my sorrows the previous day. I thought the incident would have made her understand how I felt. I was full of the confident that she would cook something to make up for the previous day. Guess what? She did not, and there were not even leftovers to eat. I lost every ounce of energy in me that very day. Was this frustrating? Yes, it was. But was I able to change my wife? Nope. Knowing full well that I cannot divorce—no retreat, no surrender—I made up my mind that I would live long and not die prematurely. So, I decided to start changing myself rather than trying to change my wife.

My wife is the recoiling type whenever there is an issue. I would rather have us address issues immediately, but she prefers to take her time. For me, why wait to sort things out and move forward; but for her, she must take her time to think about it. There was one time when we had a disagreement, and whenever we had such a misunderstanding, I was usually unable to lead in prayers. I tested her that very day, and I asked her to lead in prayers. I kid you not, she was as free as if nothing happened and truly prayed with all her heart. Right in the middle of the prayers, rather than staying focused, I was just gazing at her with surprise and had to interrupt. That action reconciled the day because she hooted in laughter when I sincerely asked her if she can teach me how she does it. I meant throwing away whatever misunderstanding and praying with a clean heart. That incident taught me to reverse my approach. So now, whenever I try for us to resolve issues and she switches into her withdrawal mode, I let go. This new approach now works well for me, unlike in the past when I used to insist we settle issues there and then, which she's never keen on doing, I'll lie wide awake with worry, starring at the ceiling at bedtime, and my wife is snoring away in a good, deep sleep.

The way she sees things differs from the way I see things. Many times, we are not on the same page. These are normal difficulties couples face every day, and it gets worst when we keep fighting to win the battle. Men are naturally born with ego. As much as I will admit that some of my wife's views over some arguments don't eventually come out right, I will also humbly admit that majority of my views don't turn out right either and have impacted more negatively on the family than hers.

I understand the importance of multiple streams of income. So, I seek new opportunities to take on to make additional income. Sometimes, when I come up with certain ideas, my wife objects to them. Back then, she was not supportive of me because of the reservations she had for some of those ideas. I went ahead with a business idea I came up with, which she did not agree with. I withdrew a large amount of money from the credit card to fund it. Eventually, the business failed, and I accumulated a huge debt for the family.

These experiences opened my eyes to a new perspective. I learned and adopted a better strategy, and that is to listen to my wife. Listening to her response when I present something to her is still a challenge because, within me, I still feel she will say something contrary. But I have learned to swallow my pride, and that's a work in progress. Things are far better now, understanding and working with my wife's personality, than in those initial early stages of our marriage. I can boldly say that I have made a tremendous improvement. I have not arrived at 100 percent; I don't think there is any man who can. The most important is that things are improving, day by day, as we stay together for better or for worse, and we are improving. The most important lesson here is understanding my wife's personality and working with it instead of trying to change her. I focused on changing my perspective, and this has helped a lot.

Comparison

My friend and I, with our wives, went out for window shopping. At the mall, my friend saw a beautiful set of dinner plates and beckoned his wife to look at them. Before we knew it, they were arguing over the dinner plates being the same set of plates he has been requesting that she buy. She had been saying they were unavailable, and behold, there they were at the mall. Right there, I compared his wife to mine, saying to him that at least his wife cooks but mine does not. I told them my request is for my wife to cook a certain kind of food, not caring about the dish or dinner plate it was served on. Though we all laughed over it, which ended their argument, I got to the point that I learned that the more I compare my wife to others, the more I missed out on the amazing strength God gave her for me.

Another friend of mine came to visit and met my wife while she was painting the walls, and I stood by the side, handing her the tools. He was amazed at what he saw because normally the roles would be reversed. Right there, he started comparing his wife to mine. These are natural errors men make, which causes most men to lose focus. Losing focus because of comparison can also lead to adultery.

> **LOSING FOCUS BECAUSE OF COMPARISON CAN ALSO LEAD TO ADULTERY.**

Communication

The volume of my speech or the depth of what I am trying to say to make my wife see and fully understand my point of view never seems to matter. I will say she is selective with what she wants to hear whenever I begin my dialogue over or after an argument or disagreement or even a rebuke. She just picks what she wants to hear and ignores the rest. She will never argue or exchange words with me. Dealing with this attitude is one of the most difficult challenges in my marriage. Then, when I do something wrong or upset her, she will never open up to talk to me about it. Most times, the only way I would sense I had done something wrong is when her mood swings to the ugly or silent direction. Sometimes, it will take me several minutes or hours to figure out exactly what I have said or done wrong. In some cases, she controls the mood swing, and I will never know what I did wrong. As I struggle to understand why my communication is not flowing well, it will keep getting worse. Why? Because I focused on how I felt, without considering how she felt as well. This issue went on until the Holy Spirit began to teach me to remove how I feel but to start focusing on how she felt. When I first started practicing this, it hurt, especially when I knew I had done nothing wrong. However, the more I practiced removing how I feel and focused on how she felt, I realized that I resolved more issues quicker and better than I used to. Letting her be, especially when she needs more time to think things over, also became a good practice that is working for me.

Prioritizing

When our three kids arrived, I could not understand how or why the attention shifted away from me. I felt lonely and excluded. All the caring and attention I usually received before the arrival of our first child disappeared overnight. The joy of those caring moments just disappeared into thin air. One day, I asked my wife why her attention is more focused on the kids, why she does not even care if I am living or not. This went on for a while until I realized that I had been missing technically as part of the family. I work full time and am engaged with a full-time ministry, so I am a "busy man." After listening to the testimony of a well-respected man of God who almost lost his marriage because of the same error I was making, it took the grace of God for me to realize that I had to re-prioritize my schedule. Now, I consciously put my family first and intentionally get involved with what goes on at home. I no longer linger after Sunday services to attend one meeting after another. My Sunday evening is now dedicated to family and fun time. We spend time together as a family and deliberate on any outstanding family issues. We play family games and partake of the Holy Communion before sharing the grace. This new habit has made a huge difference in my home. We have also factored in two or three times a year to spend quality time away as a family. It does not have to be an expensive destination—most places we visit are just neighboring states, as our family budget allows. Going to the movies occasionally is on our agenda, as well as watching them at home as a family. This bonding helps me better understand each personality, not only my wife's, but the those of the kids as well. The days of my being too busy for the family are now in the past. I can now see my wife's love is shared and balanced equally between the kids and myself.

I could go on and on with so many issues we have dealt with and are still experiencing, but as I mentioned earlier, work is still ongoing to date. I will say to all men out there, that regardless of how difficult it is to understand your wife, it is still possible to overcome these challenges in marriage. I am writing this book to let men know that quitting their marriage is not the best option. Dating around and making babies is still not the way out. I have repeatedly said that if the men remain faithful and committed to their marriages, determining that they will work by the grace of God, then the high statistics of divorce rate will fall. Having babies out of wedlock cannot be possible except for the man who decides to donate his sperm. If only men can zip up

> I WILL SAY TO ALL MEN OUT THERE, THAT REGARDLESS OF HOW DIFFICULT IT IS TO UNDERSTAND YOUR WIFE, IT IS STILL POSSIBLE TO OVERCOME THESE CHALLENGES IN MARRIAGE.

their pants and the married men stay faithful to their marriages, the community will surely get better.

I am sharing my life experience here so that others understand that it took me almost five years into our marriage to learn through the hard way. As I said, I would have chosen the easy route by saying I am no longer interested, but I stayed and was determined to work it through. Our family bonding is a work in progress and as the years go by, we learn more, experience new things, and bond better. Later in this book, I will share a few things that can help men be the real head of the family. Before that though, I will discuss mentorship in the next chapter.

Suggestion: every man needs a mentor, and every marriage needs mentorship. Mentorship helped me work through many of the issues I mentioned in this chapter.

CHAPTER TWO

MENTORSHIP

Plans fail for lack of counsel, but with many advisers they succeed.
—Proverbs 15:22

At some point during those trying periods in my marriage, I received an invitation to attend a marriage-counseling session. Immediately, it clicked that this might be what we need, although I never felt we had a problem. When a friend of mine heard that we planned on attending the marriage-counseling session, he immediately asked if we were having marital problems. My response was, "Not really." Apart from little arguments here and there, generally, my wife and I just needed to understand more about marriage. He said he was unconvinced we needed help. This reaction is typical of most men. Men feel so reluctant when it comes to such ideas. After my discussion with this friend, I almost canceled attending that marriage-counseling session, but I thank God today that I did not make that dumb decision.

My wife and I arrived at the first marriage counseling session and were warmly welcomed by the counselors who were a married couple themselves. After the introductions, the male counselor said to us that our first day of counseling would be for my wife and me to watch a movie together. I was surprised and a bit upset, as I could have stayed at home to watch the movie. He started the movie, and then he and his wife left the room. I could not stand it. I was so irritated, very impatient, and eager to leave with my wife. I thought, *how can I come for counseling and you just start a movie for me to watch.* They made matters worse by abandoning me and my wife alone to watch the movie. My wife would not let me leave and was eventually able to calm me down enough to watch it. I reluctantly agreed as the movie started. This movie captured my attention more than my wife's. As the movie went on, I realized that although I had felt we were not having any problem, it dawned on me that we did. From the beginning to the end, I saw myself in that movie, and I shed tears at the end of it. The movie itself shaped my perspective on the way I see my wife and on how self-centered I was—even before the counseling began. We later bought a few copies of that movie and gave them to a few other couples. I still recommend a movie called *Fireproof.*

Our counseling became easier because I accepted that I needed to change. During those sessions, I began to learn a lot that truly helped me adjust during our bonding stage. The marriage counselors devoted their time to us, and I remember promising them that all their efforts would not be in vain. I will not fail them, and neither will I fail God. I discussed with my wife the importance of having them be our marriage mentors. She agreed, and we approached them with the idea. We now have a couple to go to when there is a difference of view between us. We are very confident about them because they both practice what they teach. They are happily married, still living together, and have raised three godly kids. Today, all their kids are married and are still in the ministry. How else can anyone choose a mentor other than choosing people with a good track record?

Another impact from sessions with them was when they gave us a book titled *Five Love Languages* by Gary Chapman. After reading the book, I had a renewed mind. It made me realize I had not been giving my wife her love language. My wife is a gift-giving person. I never focused on that but was giving her my different love language, which is service and appreciation.

On one of my wife's birthdays, when our finances were very tight, I gave her what I thought was a great surprise without spending a lot of money. While she was out, I cleaned the entire house, washed all the dishes, and cooked a variety of dishes, including her favorite. I bought her a birthday cake and a card. I was on top of the world, nodding my head, and was so proud of myself. She came home and initially was happy with my efforts until she grabbed the birthday card, which did not have a store gift card or any gift enclosed. Meanwhile, I was lost in my own world, proud of myself and dishing out food, unaware she had left the room. I expected appreciation but did not get it. I became so frustrated and, as mentioned earlier, those were the kind of times I felt like quitting the marriage. It was during our discussion session after reading *The Five Love Languages* that my wife mentioned that scenario. I felt so ashamed of myself, but the reality is that I learned her love language. As long as it is a gift, it doesn't matter how much, as long as it is given to her, I have made her day.

Reading books that relate to raising kids, marriage, or about becoming godly men can save a lot of havoc for men. As I mentioned, most men struggle with having mentors. I might not be able to convince you to have one or even recommend one, but even just reading books can help shape you toward becoming the best husband and father your wife or kids can ever wish to have. When reading a book, you tend to connect to the author, pouring out his heart to help you get better. Just as you are reading this book, I might not be able to meet with you physically, but reading through this book will help you begin to change your perspective, and once that commences, life at home will become easier. So, I encourage you to keep reading and do not stop after this chapter.

Apart from movies and books, the practical life experiences of our mentors helped us a lot. Whenever they shared their story, it was easy for us to relate, helping us realize we were not alone. Before this, there were many things I felt I was the only one facing, but hearing this couple share their story with us made a huge impact on our marriage. At the time my wife lost her job, she felt the world had turned upside down for her. She could not help but cry most of the time. Every day, she searched for a new job. I knew it would be extremely difficult to support a family of five with just one minimum-wage income. However, deep inside of me, I felt her getting another job was not our priority. In my opinion, the kids were growing and needed more of our attention than we were able to give because of work. More so, all my wife's wages ended up as day-care fees. So, to me, it made more sense for my wife to stay at home, but I could not explain why I thought she should stop job hunting and become a stay-at-home mom to my wife. I figured that it would be the right thing for us, although it would be hard, the good thing being that she would have more time with the kids.

I could not bring myself to discuss this issue with my wife until the day our mentor came to our home with his wife for a casual visit. As they were sharing a life experience story, the wife began to narrate how she had to quit work to have more time with their kids. They were unaware that my wife had lost her job, and I never mentioned to them what was on my mind. To this day, I cannot explain why and how it happened, but my wife tapped into the idea. When they left, she asked me how I felt about her not searching for work and staying home to take care of our kids. I screamed at the top of my voice with a resounding "Yes!" Our mentors came at the right time and unknowingly resolved an issue for my wife and me in a way that I would not have been able to, should I have suggested it. I still imagine and can picture the scenario of how the discussion would have ended if it had been me that brought it up. My wife became a stay-home mom. During the time out she took to care for the kids, she enrolled for a master's degree in Clinical Psychology, completed the program, and today she is a graduate. There is nothing as beneficial as having mentorship.

A few of the issues I previously discussed in chapter one and the solutions that I gave that are working for me today are the result of mentorship received. I encourage men to find and engage with good role models. Certain things would not have worked out for me if I had not chosen to have a mentor. Marriage is an unending education. There are so many books, messages, and movies that focus on men and marriages. These materials are very helpful. Choosing a mentor is a wise idea; however, make sure the mentor has a good and Godly track record. I know of a couple that was having marital issues, and the wife found a marriage counselor. She spoke to the husband, and both went for

MARRIAGE IS AN UNENDING EDUCATION.

counseling. Unfortunately, it did not work out well the way it did for me and my wife. In the middle of the session, they asked if the counselor was married, but the counselor's response astonished them. She was a divorcee. The man convinced his wife that they should quit the session, and I indeed agree with them. You cannot give what you do not have. When choosing a counselor, please, do your background check.

Marriage Seminars

Attending marriage seminars renewed my mind for good. Most times the differences that my wife and I are battling can be resolved just by attending a marriage seminar. A few years ago, during the Christmas season, our budget was very tight. Whenever I reflect on that time, I always thank God who saw us through that period. My wife had these beautiful ideas of Christmas gifts for our kids, close family members, and friends. Naturally, I am a cheerful giver, but when it comes to giving at very difficult times, I do my math very well. Do not get me wrong, I believe in sacrificial giving and still practice it today. However, when it comes to the type of giving my wife was planning, I like to stay within what we have and not spend what we do not have.

So as usual, disagreement kicked in. My wife felt it was ideal to spend a certain amount of money by simply putting it on a credit card. I felt it did not make sense filling the credit card just to put smiles on people's faces while struggling to pay an unending minimum fee. She insisted that she should still do what she had already planned. Well, never expect to win such battles. Learn not to have the last word when in such arguments. As the head of the family, swallow your pride and let go. Experiences have taught me that the best place to win such arguments is to go on the knees in prayer. I will share how to win such conflicting issues by taking it to the Lord in prayers much later in this book, but for now, I will re-focus attention on me and my wife attending a marriage seminar.

We arrived at the marriage seminar not at peace because of our miscommunication. For me, it takes only the grace of God to have me settled and yes, the Lord did just that. While the minister was going through the message for the day, without knowing what we argued about, he began to deal with the issue standing between us. Guess what? Financial management was the major topic we dealt with in that session. Afterward, thank God, my wife withdrew from going ahead with her wish. The minister echoed all that I had been saying, but my wife heard it clearer, as it was coming from someone else. Men, I have no doubt some of you have found yourselves in similar situations, where you say something and your wife abandons it, but once it comes from another person, she gets it. You are not alone, and that is why I always recommend marriage seminars. Listening to people with good track records teaching words of wisdom goes a long way as a great mentorship. Can you imagine what could have happened if we never attended that marriage seminar session?

Men's Gatherings

> *As iron sharpens iron, so one person sharpens another.* (Prov. 27:17)

Men do have a lot going on that our nature prevents us from confiding in others. But men gathering for fellowship helps. When men gather, they pour out their hearts to encourage one another. You never know how good your home is until you hear another brother's struggle in his home. When we share and encourage one another, the final quest is to pray for one another as we continue leading our families.

At one of our men's gathering, a man walked up to me and thanked me for starting such a wonderful leadership fellowship that is focused on men. He and his wife, according to him, on that fateful day, had decided to separate. He said he was so down and weak inside that, although he had thought of so many silly things to do, he remembered our fellowship. That day, the minister was preaching about issues that seemed personal to him and that broke him. Yes, never twist it; men do cry! Men in most cases keep it real when they are alone with fellow men. So, upon resonation with the sermon, he decided to apologize and make up with his wife as it dawned on him that he is the problem in his marriage and not his wife. Now, for such a caliber of man, he would not have naturally yielded to mentorship from any person or attended a marriage seminar with his wife. Getting into and attending men's fellowship gave him the right mentorship that helped him. Today, he is still happily married to his wife and at home with the kids.

Good Friendship

I have mentioned good friendship because most men also do have wrong friends. The wrong set of friends can and often will cause you to lose your home. I have heard the story of a young man who was having issues with the wife. This young man met with his friends at their regular drinking bar and talked about his marital issues. His friends of course advised him wrongly and, acting on their advice, caused him to be kicked out of his home by law enforcement agents. When he arrived at one of his friend's houses unannounced, he saw the friend on bended knees begging his wife to forgive him on whatever the issue was that they had. Asking or begging for forgiveness from a wife, was something they had advised him against doing. Can you imagine, how bad advice can impact people negatively? What the friends advised this young man to do was the very opposite of what he witnessed when he arrived at his friend's home.

When you surround yourself with godly men, whose integrity is tested, you will be influenced by their good deeds. I am blessed to have such men surround me, and I am blessed living the life I see them live. One of them invited me to spend a few hours with him. During the time spent together, he shared with me the mistakes he has made in life as a man and how to avoid making them myself. What a friend indeed. There is no greater mentorship than having people who are willing to open up to you and share their mistakes and advise you on how to navigate away from making the same mistake.

Today, I join others who have the passion for encouraging men to live up to the standard our creator designed, that we men should lead the family. We are the head and should do everything possible to live up to the standard. By the special grace of God, I see myself being transparent to close friends of mine as well. Men, we are in this together, and together we all shall reduce the statistics of absent fathers at home. This can be achieved when we all gather knowledge and apply that knowledge to our lives and others. Together we shall make all homes function as designed and directed by God.

CHAPTER THREE

VISION

Where there is no revelation, people cast off restraint;
but blessed is the one who heeds wisdom's instruction.
—Proverbs 29:18

There is no greater need today in our society than visionary men leading their families in the right direction. We are witnessing the absence of fathers in the home because most men either have lost the vision or do not even know what the vision is all about. A lot of the negative impact, as reflected in the statistics quoted in introducing this book, results from men without a vision. When a man has no vision, the family collapses. How do we rediscover or know what the vision is? We need to go back to the original intent of our Creator.

Work

This is the account of the heavens and the earth when they were created when the Lord God made the earth and the heavens. Now no shrub had yet appeared on the earth and no plant had yet sprung up, for the Lord God had not sent rain on the earth and there was no one to work the ground, but streams came up from the earth and watered the whole surface of the ground. Then the Lord God formed a man from the dust of the ground and breathed into his nostrils the breath of life, and the man became a living being. (Gen. 2:4–7)

The very first reason God formed a man is for work. There was no one to work the ground, and God created a man to do the work. So, the primary responsibility for every man is to understand the vision behind our being the head of our families. It is that we should work. Many men prefer to be the head and wear the title of the head of the family but refuse to work.

Work here means toil. Before a man thinks of a woman to marry, he, first, must secure work or be engaged in some daily activity that earns him

> **THE VERY FIRST REASON GOD FORMED A MAN IS FOR WORK.**

a living. A man without a steady source of income is not qualified to marry. That is the vision, and men need to rediscover this vision; otherwise, homes will keep collapsing. Being engaged in work has nothing, and I repeat, nothing, to do with how much you earn. It's all about fulfilling the primary purpose of being the head of the family. When a man is working, he is fulfilling the original intent of how God designed him to be.

Manage

> *The Lord God took the man and put him in the Garden of Eden to work it and take care of it.* (Gen. 2:15)

It was repeated in Genesis 2:15 of the Holy Bible that a man was formed to work. However, something was added. God's intent is not just for the man to work but also to be a manager. Every man must be an excellent manager. There is no better place to manage things other than managing himself well and the affairs of his home. A man who cannot manage his affairs is not qualified to marry yet. Successfully managing affairs here includes having a shelter over his head, a place he returns to for rest, a home to go to. A home as described here does not need to be the American dream home. It can even be a studio, but he must possess a home that he is managing. He should first be able to clean his home, do laundry, dishes, and maintain the lawn, and so on before we can consider him qualified. If he does all this, you find out that it will never be a burdensome task to do the same when the helper (wife) arrives. Being an excellent manager is not a position in the workplace. We have many instances where we have good managers at workplaces who are terrible at managing their own homes. God created everything, and everything He created was good. There is a reason He went through this creation process before introducing the woman. Men must reconnect to the original purpose, renewing their minds with the vision of being the head of their family before the actual head of the family will emerge.

Instruction

And the Lord God commanded the man, "You are free to eat from any tree in the garden; but you must not eat from the tree of the knowledge of good and evil, for when you eat from it you will certainly die." (Gen. 2:16–17)

After God formed man to work and manage, the next step was for man to receive instruction on how to manage. Management of your home should not be based solely on how you think or feel it should be done. There are always specific instructions

THE KNOWLEDGE YOU HAVE AND THE APPLICATION OF THAT KNOWLEDGE MAKES YOU A VISIONARY HEAD. NOT EVEN A RICH MAN CAN BE COMPARED TO A MAN OF VISION.

given that will help a man be the head that will lead his family in the right direction. That is why a man must have equipped himself with these three stages in his life before taking on marriage. Instructions are important to build up a man into maturity. It takes more than exercise and nutrition for you to become a visionary head. The knowledge you have and the application of that knowledge makes you a visionary head. Not even a rich man can be compared to a man of vision. Be patient with a man of vision, and the end will amaze you.

Completion

The Lord God said, "It is not good for the man to be alone. I will make a helper suitable for him." (Gen. 2:18)

A man is not complete and can never be until there is a helper suitable for him. So, a woman comes into a man's life to help him fulfill God's vision. The woman comes in to help the man work, manage and execute the instructions God gave. When we follow these

> A MAN IS NOT COMPLETE AND CAN NEVER BE UNTIL THERE IS A HELPER SUITABLE FOR HIM. SO, A WOMAN COMES INTO A MAN'S LIFE TO HELP HIM FULFILL GOD'S VISION.

simple principles, the headship role becomes loving and not authoritative. Women are in men's lives to help them become complete and fulfill their original purpose.

So, a woman saying, "I do," must say that to a man who is already working, managing his home, and has specific instructions he can present to the woman. Riches may dwindle, six-pack muscles may disappear, but a visionary man moves from glory to glory and from strength to strength. That is why whenever a suitable helper comes into the life of a visionary man, within a brief period, the glory manifests.

Man of Vision

You may now be asking how do I reconnect to become a visionary man, or you would like to become a visionary man. Below are practical steps you need to cultivate to develop and see amazing joy within yourself, no matter if you are single or married.

Personal Altar

For a man to be a visionary head, there must be a specific time for prayers. Praying is communicating with the Lord. It should be a daily process, a way of life rather than a random or infrequent event. When men pray, it draws them closer to the Lord, and the closer men are to the Lord, the more they hear from Him. One word from the Lord can change or turn anything around for good. In this twentieth century, the number of men who are in the habit of praying has reduced drastically, and that is why men are losing their headship.

Reading

Men need the wisdom to run their homes, and they can achieve this by reading the right books. Reading the Bible is the primary source of receiving sound instructions that can make men wise if they put the knowledge they gained into practice. Motivational books of a positive nature should also be read. Every man should be a reader because readers make brilliant leaders.

Meditation

Meditating to hear the Lord speak is so vital for men. Most men are inpatient, and this affects their capacity to receive a word from God. Men must create time to meditate, especially after reading the Bible and receiving sound messages. The more men meditate, the better they become.

Discipline

Becoming a visionary head requires developing self-discipline. When you receive certain instructions, it requires self-discipline to attain it. Proper vision requires discipline. A man will never lose focus when he develops a disciplined life. Praying daily, reading the Bible and Christian books, and meditating require discipline—he must overcome all kinds of distractions that would surely take him off track. Becoming a visionary head requires discipline.

Vision Cast

Casting the vision should be a yearly exercise for every man. The vision should comprise of what you have heard the Lord say, things you are expecting the Lord to do, goals you wish to attain, and how to attain those goals. Put them down in writing, cast them in such a way that they should attract the family to align with it. If single, develop the habit and cast the vision yearly to help guide you.

Transparent

There should be nothing in hiding. A visionary head will not have passwords that could prevent the wife from accessing his electronic devices, especially phones. All passwords or codes should be made known to each other. Communication should be clear with no hidden agenda. I do not get it when I hear ladies complaining that their men will not allow them to have access to their gadgets. Visionary heads are transparent in all things.

Financial Management

Visionary heads must always have their finances in mind. I mentioned earlier that it is not about how much you earn but how much effort you put into your work. Here, there must be a sound financial management plan. A visionary head seeks and exercises sound judgment when it comes to finances. Debts of the family should be of huge concern, and it should be his burden on how to eradicate the debts and seek financial freedom for the home. He must not add to the problem but, rather, act to solve the problem.

Myths

> *Anyone who does not provide for their relatives, and especially for their own household, has denied the faith and is worse than an unbeliever.* (1 Tim. 5:8)

I do not know how this scripture got twisted, but the misinterpretation of this verse has crippled a lot of men who either lost their job or who are making less than their wives. Remember, we discussed that the original intent is for a man to work. It has nothing to do with how much a man earns. The verse is not addressing those who may have lost their jobs. It is addressing the idle man who chooses not to work.

She does not respect me because she earns more than I do

I will keep emphasizing this because it has ruined many men and homes. Being visionary is more important than earning more money than your wife. Women have issues with men without vision. Where there is a vision, everything falls in line. It is not all about money. I have seen instances where the man earns more than enough, and yet, the marriage struggles. When you query the man, the response is the usual "she doesn't respect me." What matters more to the women is not how much you are making but where you are leading the family.

Wives, submit yourselves to your own husbands as you do to the Lord. (Eph. 5:22)

You hear most men quote this scripture out of context. The funny part is that they quote this scripture neglecting, to start from the verse before that says:

Submit to one another out of reverence for Christ. (Eph. 5:21)

Paul was addressing the household with his instruction, telling the men and the women to submit to one another regarding their obligations in reverence for Christ. Visionary heads submit to their wives by fulfilling their obligation, which is to love their wives regardless of whether their wives are submissive to them.

Husbands, love your wives, just as Christ loved the church and gave himself up for her. (Eph. 5:25)

Most men focus on their rights, which is why they only see that the wife is not submissive. But the visionary head should focus on their obligation to love their wives. Remember, visionary men are filled with instructions from God; knowing what to do and doing what they know. They love their wives unconditionally. The moment a man says his wife is not submissive, that man has lost it.

Joint bank accounts instead of separate accounts

Visionary heads should strive to have joint bank accounts with their spouses rather than separate accounts. This helps eliminate unnecessary competition and inferiority complex among couples, especially where the man earns less. If a man should leave his parent to unite with the wife, both should have things in common.

> *That is why a man leaves his father and mother and is united to his wife, and they become one flesh.* (Gen. 2:24)

To have both the man and woman as managers at the same time is not right. Remember in the introduction, man becomes the head (first) to manage, and thereafter God brought the woman to be a co-manager. So, if in a home, the woman is considered the better manager, she should manage the account rather than the man. Managing the family account should never be based on who is making more money. Having a joint family bank account should not prevent individuals from having personal accounts. Family accounts deal with general family savings, expenses, and investment, while individual accounts deal with individual needs.

> *To the woman he said, "I will make your pains in childbearing very severe; with painful labor you will give birth to children. Your desire will be for your husband, and he will rule over you."* (Gen. 3:16)

Here is another scripture that is often twisted and misused. Many men have quoted this scripture to intimidate their spouses and position themselves as more superior. They manipulate and dominate their spouses because to them, their wives are under them. They feel that men rule. This scripture is a curse decreed by God because of the downfall of mankind. However, in today's dispensation, we no longer live under the curse because Jesus Christ paid the price for us. Those men who manipulate and dominate their wives should consider themselves still living under the curse. Little wonder why those men who mistreat their wives struggle to live rather than enjoying life by grace.

To Adam he said, "Because you listened to your wife and ate fruit from the tree about which I commanded you, 'You must not eat from it,' Cursed is the ground because of you; through painful toil you will eat food from it all the days of your life. It will produce thorns and thistles for you, and you will eat the plants of the field." (Gen. 3:17–18)

Every visionary head operates under the grace of God, knowing well that Christ paid the price. They neither manipulate nor dominate their wives. They know that both males and females are the same, spiritually and physically. God created them male and female out of His image. The woman is a helper, but equal, and should be nurtured with care and unconditional love.

CHAPTER FOUR

FAITHFUL

Most men will proclaim everyone his own goodness,
but a faithful man who can find?
—Proverbs 20:6

There are a lot of men out there claiming to have unfailing love, but their actions prove the opposite of whom they claim to be, causing many marriages to be in shambles today. There are many instances of men deceiving women, claiming to be what they are not and tricking them into marriage. In most instances, such marriages do not last. The negative statistics on divorce keep rising, and the absence of a father remains an inevitable factor. Some men, when they want to get married, will wear the cloth of a faithful man in the church. Their intention is just to wow that godly woman. A short time after they are married, their true personality manifests. Many women who enter a marriage based on such deceit soon start seeing so many things they never thought or would believe the man is capable of. Authentic life stories include the woman who is lamenting and crying for help because she never knew the man was an alcoholic or that he smokes or was into drugs. Some women discover that men have lied about their bad debts and never disclosed such debts until after the marriage and the woman discovers the situation by herself. Some men lie about their jobs. Often a man is married and will lie about that relationship, just to get into a new one. This occurrence is very prevalent among immigrants. They may have a family at their place of origin and then hide or lie about that fact. Sometimes they will then enter a new marriage in order to obtain citizenship. I can go on and on with examples of such true-life stories. Again, most of these deceitful marriages end up in divorce and contribute to the rising rate of absent fathers at home. Having said all this, the question will now be (*but a faithful man who can find*? (Prov. 20:6b).

Faithful

In chapter three, we read about vision. Vision comes when a man draws close to his Creator and receives instructions. Faithfulness starts when a man becomes obedient to the word of God. A faithful head of the family is, therefore, that man who after receiving instructions from God becomes obedient to those instructions. Out of the love a man has for God, he positions himself to faithfully carry out God's instructions

> VISION COMES WHEN A MAN DRAWS CLOSE TO HIS CREATOR AND RECEIVES INSTRUCTIONS. FAITHFULNESS STARTS WHEN A MAN BECOMES OBEDIENT TO THE WORD OF GOD. A FAITHFUL HEAD OF THE FAMILY IS, THEREFORE, THAT MAN WHO AFTER RECEIVING INSTRUCTIONS FROM GOD BECOMES OBEDIENT TO THOSE INSTRUCTIONS.

without compromise. As we discussed in chapter one, this includes having a personal altar (time of prayers). His discipline in reading, meditation, vision casting, being transparent, and financial management are faithfully put into practice. He becomes dedicated and committed to carrying out these positive habits. Please keep in mind that these are just a few examples as they relate to the purpose of this book.

Test of Faith

When a man becomes committed to obeying the word of God, God Himself will test his faithfulness.

The LORD God said, "It is not good for the man to be alone. I will make a helper suitable for him." Now the LORD God had formed out of the ground all the wild animals and all the birds in the sky. He brought them to the man to see what he would name them; and whatever the man called each living creature, that was its name. So, the man gave names to all the livestock, the birds in the sky and all the wild animals. But for Adam no suitable helper was found. (Gen. 2:18–20)

Note that when God said, "It is not good for a man to be alone," He did not bring a woman. Instead, He brought to man the living creatures to see what he would name them. Adam carried out the assignment faithfully, committing no sin. He just named them, remaining faithful, waiting for the suitable helper. It was at that passing of the test that God now brought the woman into the picture.

So the LORD God caused the man to fall into a deep sleep; and while he was sleeping, he took one of the man's ribs and then closed up the place with flesh. Then the LORD God made a woman from the rib he had taken out of the man, and he brought her to the man. The man said, "This is now bone of my bones and flesh of my flesh; she shall be called 'woman,' for she was taken out of man." (Gen. 2:21–23)

Patience

The faithful head of the family strives to be patient in all circumstances. We saw this in the account of Adam. He faithfully carried out his assignment and waited patiently for God. We can compare this to our lives today. Faithful heads patiently keep themselves pure and holy until they wed their right spouse. I always advise young men to abstain from fornication during courtship. Dating a lady to prepare for becoming married is approved. However, there must not be a submission to the temptation of premarital sex. Ladies should observe that a faithful man will never rush her into

FAITHFUL HEADS PATIENTLY KEEP THEMSELVES PURE AND HOLY UNTIL THEY WED THEIR RIGHT SPOUSE.

having sex until they are married. So, when a man is not patient enough to wait, it is a red flag. I am writing this book to create more awareness for men to learn how to be patient and abstain from sex. If we disciple more faithful men, the number of absent fathers will be reduced in our communities. Faithful men wait for their wives patiently at the grocery shops or malls. I must confess that I do always remind myself that I will do all I can by the grace of God to exercise patience while waiting for my wife at the grocery store. Most men are impatient, but this should never be an excuse to break God's principles. Again, that is the reason God tested Adam. Impatience has led men into so many calamities in their lives. When things are not going as hoped for, as in the promises of God, wait patiently until it manifests.

Marriage

Faithful heads remain faithful to their wives. It is a covenant made and they stick to it.

May your fountain be blessed, and may you rejoice in the wife of your youth. A loving doe, a graceful deer - may her breasts satisfy you always, may you ever be intoxicated with her love. (Prov. 5:18–19)

There is no interest in cheating because God gives suitable helpers to each man and the faithful are satisfied with their own. The faithful man also makes a covenant with their eyes not to look at women with lust, especially in

FAITHFUL HEADS REMAIN FAITHFUL TO THEIR WIVES. IT IS A COVENANT MADE, AND THEY STICK TO IT.

our generation, where dressing indecently is tolerated as modern fashion. Job made such a covenant, and all faithful men should make the same covenant.

I made a covenant with my eyes not to look lustfully at a young woman. (Job 31:1)

Integrity

Faithful heads are men of integrity. According to the Cambridge dictionary, integrity means the quality of being honest and having strong

FAITHFUL HEADS ARE MEN OF INTEGRITY.

moral principles. When a man is honest, the wife goes to sleep whenever he is not at home. The wife trusts him for who he is. I always tell people they do not really know who I am until they ask my wife. It is extremely hard for a man of integrity to compromise his moral principles. He cannot be bought with money, even if he lacks money.

Servant Leader

Faithful heads are men that serve their families. When Jesus addressed the real meaning of servant leadership, He specified it very clearly.

FAITHFUL HEADS ARE MEN WHO SERVE THEIR FAMILIES.

Jesus called them together and said, "You know that the rulers of the Gentiles lord it over them, and their high officials exercise authority over them. Not so with you. Instead, whoever wants to become great among you must be your servant." (Matt. 20:25–26)

Being the head of the family truly positions you to serve your family without grumbling. Most men find it difficult to do household chores, such as cooking, laundry, dishes, lawn mowing, and cleaning up. I call the act of not trying to help with domestic chores "irresponsible," and it contributes to divorce in some homes. If men who are called to be the head would understand that being the head means to serve their family, the numbers of absent fathers would be drastically reduced.

Availability

It is one thing to understand the role of being the head, which puts you in the position to serve your family, but it is a different thing altogether when you are not available at home to carry out your assignment as the head. Many men become so busy at work they neglect their duties at home. There is great importance to being available at home. The presence of a father at home matters a lot. I remember when my first son was about three years old. He had so much energy for jumping and littering the living room. On

> IT IS ONE THING TO UNDERSTAND THE ROLE OF BEING THE HEAD, WHICH PUTS YOU IN THE POSITION TO SERVE YOUR FAMILY, BUT IT IS A DIFFERENT THING ALTOGETHER WHEN YOU ARE NOT AVAILABLE AT HOME TO CARRY OUT YOUR ASSIGNMENT AS THE HEAD.

this one day, he was doing his usual, and his mother kept shouting and calling him to calm down, but he kept on. I sat right there watching with interest and thinking of the most appropriate disciplinary action to take. But my wife did something that remains fresh in my mind. She just said to him, "OK, I will tell your dad." My son heard what she said, and he immediately stopped. He then realized I was right there in the living room, and he rushed toward me and hugged me. Now, why did he not stop at the initial caution from his mom? Why did he yield to the instruction only at the mention of telling Dad? Again, rushing to me with a hug seems smart on his side, but it also sends me the message that the presence of fathers at home makes an immense difference.

Unconditional Love

I repeat this statement over and over in this book. I intend that it be clarified that, by His grace, men should love their wives unconditionally. This

> BY HIS GRACE, MEN SHOULD LOVE THEIR WIVES UNCONDITIONALLY.

act does not require the wives to respect or always agree with the head. It means the head should love the wife unconditionally, even if they do not return it. Faithful men strive to love unconditionally because of their understanding that when we love our wives unconditionally, we are honoring God and are in good standing with our Creator. This kind of unconditional love should also extend to the children. If this registers in the heart of men, there will not be any room for giving up. I call it: "No retreat, no surrender." Never give up on your wife, and never give up on your kids, even in inevitable situations. I understand how upset you are reading this if you are a man, but I advise you to keep the love unconditional and, by God's grace, you shall overcome. We will discuss more later in this book about overcoming via the powers of prayers.

Forgiveness

A lot of scripture deals with forgiveness. In most situations, we choose the ones to forgive and the ones not to forgive. The truth remains that we ought to forgive as often as possible. When this is in our hearts, most of the divorce cases can be resolved through forgiveness and reconciliation without ending in divorce, which keeps increasing the rate of absent fathers at home. Faithful men take the lead to forgive, even when they feel they are right. Remember, it is not about being right but about being faithful to the Creator. Unforgiveness hinders prayers, and faithful men are the priests of the home. Never insist on not forgiving. The Bible mentions we must honor our wives as the weaker vessel so our prayers will not be hindered.

> FAITHFUL MEN TAKE THE LEAD TO FORGIVE, EVEN WHEN THEY FEEL THEY ARE RIGHT. REMEMBER, IT IS NOT ABOUT BEING RIGHT BUT ABOUT BEING FAITHFUL TO THE CREATOR.

> *Husbands, in the same way be considerate as you live with your wives, and treat them with respect as the weaker partner and as heirs with you of the gracious gift of life, so that nothing will hinder your prayers.* (1 Pet. 3:7)

Faithful men should understand they are wired differently from their spouses. What a man can overlook within a second might take a woman some few minutes to overlook. Faithful men should always be the first to initiate forgiveness and to reconcile.

The same applies to how we deal with our children. Faithful men should always be prepared to forgive their children, knowing that they will always act childishly. A faithful man never disowns his child or stays away from his children. As you read the story of the prodigal son in the Bible extract below, you will realize that no matter what a child does, when he returns, as a faithful man, there's always room to forgive and give that child a second chance.

Jesus continued: "There was a man who had two sons. The younger one said to his father, 'Father, give me my share of the estate.' So he divided his property between them. Not long after that, the younger son got together all he had, set off for a distant country and there squandered his wealth in wild living. After he had spent everything, there was a severe famine in that whole country, and he began to be in need. So he went and hired himself out to a citizen of that country, who sent him to his fields to feed pigs. He longed to fill his stomach with the pods that the pigs were eating, but no one gave him anything. When he came to his senses, he said, 'How many of my father's hired servants have food to spare, and here I am starving to death! I will set out and go back to my father and say to him: Father, I have sinned against heaven and against you. I am no longer worthy to be called your son; make me like one of your hired servants.' So he got up and went to his father. But while he was still a long way off, his father saw him and was filled with compassion for him; he ran to his son, threw his arms around him and kissed him. The son said to him, 'Father, I have sinned against heaven and against you. I am no longer worthy to be called your son.' "But the father said to his servants, 'Quick! Bring the best robe and put it on him. Put a ring on his finger and sandals on his feet. Bring the fattened calf and kill it. Let's have a feast and celebrate. For this son of mine was dead and is alive again; he was lost and is found.' So they began to celebrate."
(Luke 15:11–24)

CHAPTER 5

PRIESTHOOD

When a period of feasting had run its course, Job would make arrangements for them to be purified. Early in the morning he would sacrifice a burnt offering for each of them, thinking, "Perhaps my children have sinned and cursed God in their hearts." This was Job's regular custom.
—Job 1:5

Growing up, it was normal for my mom to take the lead in ensuring we were regular in attending Sunday services, midweek services, or any church program. I believed it is a normal duty for mothers. Is this how it should be? Well, most families I saw while growing up had mothers play the lead role in calling for family prayers or attending any church event, but I realize that this is against the original plan of our creator. I learned the truth at a later stage in my life, which was when I surrendered my life to Christ.

FROM THE BEGINNING, GOD HAD GIVEN THE PRIESTHOOD ROLE TO THE MAN TO LEAD THE FAMILY WHILE THE WIFE ASSISTS HIM.

From the beginning, God had given the priesthood role to the man to lead the family while the wife assists him. Remember, He meant for the man to fill the responsibility role, and the woman took on the assisting role. Having read the Bible, it occurred to me that the original

37

plan was for every man to be the priest of his own home. The priesthood role is a major responsibility expected of a man by God. If men rise to occupy this role, there will be a shifting in heaven's intervention. I will never be against the calling and anointing of women. I am talking about the divine order. No one can change the divine order and have a peaceful home. Many women who God is using today understand the divine order and concede the priesthood role to the man in their home.

One reason many men lose their families is because of their lack of understanding and not filling the role of a priest in their homes. The priesthood role helps men draw closer to God and to get more involved with their families. It is an office of intercession, the watchman of the family. The above scripture in Job 1:5 recorded how Job prayed for his children in case they had sinned. The priest is the man who communicates with God, asking for daily direction for

> ONE REASON MANY MEN LOSE THEIR FAMILIES IS BECAUSE OF THEIR LACK OF UNDERSTANDING AND NOT FILLING THE ROLE OF A PRIEST IN THEIR HOMES. THE PRIESTHOOD ROLE HELPS MEN DRAW CLOSER TO GOD AND TO GET MORE INVOLVED WITH THEIR FAMILIES. IT IS AN OFFICE OF INTERCESSION, THE WATCHMAN OF THE FAMILY.

his family. Again, every man needs to hear from God and to see clearly what God is saying concerning his family. Many men have made incorrect decisions that have ruined their families. We enjoy the grace of God today because of the complete work of our Lord Jesus Christ, yet that grace did not take away the consequences that follow any wrong decision men make for their family. In most cases, the consequences of making a poor decision may affect everyone in the family. Let us read about one incorrect move and the consequences of that man's wrong decision-making.

> *In the days when the judges ruled, there was a famine in the land. So a man from Bethlehem in Judah, together with his wife and two sons, went to live for a while in the country of Moab. The man's name was Elimelek,*

his wife's name was Naomi, and the names of his two sons were Mahlon and Kilion. They were Ephrathites from Bethlehem, Judah. And they went to Moab and lived there.

Now Elimelek, Naomi's husband, died, and she was left with her two sons. They married Moabite women, one named Orpah and the other Ruth. After they had lived there about ten years, both Mahlon and Kilion also died, and Naomi was left without her two sons and her husband. (Ruth 1:1–5)

We need to understand that the consequences of how making a wrong decision can affect our families. Elimelek, who left his country to go to another because of famine, lost his own life. The aftermath of his decision to move left his wife, Naomi, without a husband. Later, her two sons also died, leaving her alone as a widow. As an immigrant, I know and have heard of so many stories that negatively affected many families because they migrated from their country of origin to another country.

Many have even lost their lives during the journey to the unknown land. Some arrive in an unfamiliar country, and because they cannot bring over the family they left behind, they begin new families. This is evident today, as we have many men who left their families in their country of origin and are now married afresh in their new country of residence. Can you imagine the struggle left over for such abandoned women and kids? Can you imagine how the children must suffer and what they will become as they grow up without their father or perhaps not knowing who their father is?

Responsibilities of a Priesthood
Study

Do your best to present yourself to God as one approved, a worker who does not need to be ashamed and who correctly handles the word of truth. (2 Tim. 2:15)

This is so vital for every man who wants to be the head of his family. Men ought to study to show themselves approved by God. We cannot understand the original purpose or the plan of marriage without reading and studying the Bible. The nonchalant attitude of not studying the Bible has caused more harm than good to our families. When men fail to study, they lack the knowledge to be the head needed at home. And when this happens, guess

MEN OUGHT TO STUDY TO SHOW THEMSELVES APPROVED BY GOD.

what? The wife and children get leadership from the so-called false prophets operating everywhere. I have witnessed cases where men complain that their wives pay more attention to the pastors than they do to their own ideas. Well, a woman will not naturally agree with a man who doesn't draw his ideas from the Lord. Like I mentioned in the previous chapter, men need to be aware of study materials that will add value to their lives—enough of slacking around and being busy with things that do not matter. I am not against watching movies, sports channels, news channels, or reading magazines, but we ought to make our choices and wisely manage our time. We can do all the mentioned activities, but we must reserve time to study God's word by reading the Bible and other God-honoring motivational books, studies, and programs. Have a yearly goal of reading through the Bible and reading at least one book that will add value to daily living every month. When we seek to study and apply the knowledge we gather, the headship in the family becomes easier and peaceful.

Teach

Only be careful and watch yourselves closely so that you do not forget the things your eyes have seen or let them fade from your heart as long as you live. Teach them to your children and to their children after them. (Deut. 4:9)

This comes naturally from studying. As a priest of the family, the more you study, the more you attain the knowledge to teach and pass on to future generations. Nothing can beat the memory of teaching the family the knowledge gained from your studies. When our families hear the word of truth spoken in the home, the impact remains strong on the kids as they grow. Again, what you fail to teach them will be taught by the many wolves out there in the camouflage of a pastor. When my first son turned twelve years old, I decided we would spend some time together for us to bond and to allow him to start to feel like a grown man. I will never forget one question he asked me at an early age. In his own words, he innocently asked, "Daddy, is there anything wrong in

> AS A PRIEST OF THE FAMILY, THE MORE YOU STUDY, THE MORE YOU ATTAIN THE KNOWLEDGE TO TEACH AND PASS ON TO FUTURE GENERATIONS. NOTHING CAN BEAT THE MEMORY OF TEACHING THE FAMILY THE KNOWLEDGE GAINED FROM YOUR STUDIES.

having a girlfriend?" I must confess that at first, I was thrown off balance because I was not expecting such a question. My background did not help issues either, because as an African, and back in the days of my childhood, such a question, especially from a child, would have been deemed forbidden. But thank God that by His grace, I had genuine answers to offer. I believe I addressed the question sufficiently to his level of understanding. I know you are curious about what my answer to that question was. Well, do not be because I only mentioned it here for you to understand that it is our role to teach and guide our families wisely.

> *Start children off on the way they should go, and even when they are old they will not turn from it.* (Prov. 22:6)

Prayers

The personal prayer altar is where we communicate to God and present issues. Most of our battles are won via prayers. Cultivating the habit of waking up early and praying first thing in the morning changes our lifestyle and positively affects our decision-making. I want to comment that if there are areas that seem impossible to handle, especially in our relationship with our spouses, taking our concerns and desires to the Lord in prayer yields amazing results. Stop fighting physically and begin to fight spiritually. I have been blessed to share this truth with the many men that I have had the privilege to mentor. It has helped them stop making the

> **STOP FIGHTING PHYSICALLY AND BEGIN TO FIGHT SPIRITUALLY.**

mistake of trying to change their wives. No one can change another person except God. I encourage men never to give up or quit just because something seems impossible. It might be impossible with men, but not with God. Prayer time is the best time to communicate with God, a time to listen and to hear God.

Listening

It is especially important to understand that listening is an essential role the head of the family assumes. I mentioned it briefly in chapter one, but I will explain in more detail why it is a very vital role for the priest of the family.

> **IT IS ESPECIALLY IMPORTANT TO UNDERSTAND THAT LISTENING IS AN ESSENTIAL ROLE THE HEAD OF THE FAMILY ASSUMES.**

During prayers, when you communicate, listen to hear God speak. I recently learned this, and it works perfectly for me. I cannot tell you how many times I have prayerfully presented to God the issues that I felt were right. Listening during devotion has helped me hear God speak clearly that I am on the wrong path. One such time was when my wife and I had excellent reason to believe it was time for us to buy a home. We did our pre-approval and had an agent working with us. We had looked at homes for sale that we admired, and we were on the verge of buying. But during one of my prayer times, as I was listening to hear God speak, I heard loud and clear that it was not yet time to buy. It made little sense to me at the time, and I struggled to share the news with my wife. I thank God we yielded to His instruction. We canceled our plans to purchase a house, and a few months after we made that decision, my wife lost her job. One word heard from God can make a huge difference in our lives.

Listening to our wives is also very crucial if we want to fulfill God's plan and purpose in our families. I have shared how when I ignored my wife's counsel, I brought

ONE WORD HEARD FROM GOD CAN MAKE A HUGE DIFFERENCE IN OUR LIVES.

pain to my family. I am deeply passionate about commenting on this because many men bring havoc upon their homes just because they refused to listen to their wives. While reading Ruth, chapter 1, I kept imaging what if Naomi had advised her husband, contrary to his wish of them migrating to another country, and perhaps he refused? I have paid the price several times for not following my wife's advice. I am writing to encourage other men—many times God speaks through our wives. Regardless of how spiritual we might think we are, God speaks through our wives. If we learn to listen to our wives, we will avoid unnecessary mistakes and move into God's divine plan. The story of Abraham and Sarah is a typical example to share here. I am sure that if God had not intervened, Abraham would not have listened to Sarah.

LISTENING TO OUR WIVES IS ALSO VERY CRUCIAL IF WE WANT TO FULFILL GOD'S PLAN AND PURPOSE IN OUR FAMILIES.

The child grew and was weaned, and on the day Isaac was weaned Abraham held a great feast. But Sarah saw that the son whom Hagar the Egyptian had borne to Abraham was mocking, and she said to Abraham, "Get rid of that slave woman and her son, for that woman's son will never share in the inheritance with my son Isaac." The matter distressed Abraham greatly because it concerned his son. But God said to him, "Do not be so distressed about the boy and your slave woman. Listen to whatever Sarah tells you, because it is through Isaac that your offspring will be reckoned. I will make the son of the slave into a nation also, because he is your offspring." (Gen. 21:8–13)

Listening to our children is also important.

In the last days, God says, "I will pour out my Spirit on all people. Your sons and daughters will prophesy, your young men will see visions, your old men will dream dreams." (Acts 2:17)

During the period I previously mentioned, I had this wonderful plan to purchase a two-bedroom ranch home and later finish the basement. Right in the middle of that plan, someone offered my wife and me the exact specifications of my ideal plan. My wife had no issues with the plan; all she wanted was a suitable home that would accommodate our family of five. We had not discussed these plans with our children. My oldest son woke up one morning and shared his dream about the negative consequences awaiting us if we embarked on our plan. I have paid my dues for not listening to my wife, so wisdom required that I pay attention. God is still in the business of talking to us daily. He is a merciful God. When we miss his voice, He speaks either through our wives or our children. Never be too sure or adamant to ignore the advice of your spouse or children. I had every reason to ignore my son's dream. I would have thought it was just an ordinary dream from a child but, thank God, I yielded to that dream, which was a vision.

Intercessor

"Perhaps my children have sinned and cursed God in their hearts." This was Job's regular custom. (Job 1:5)

Pray for your family always. Step into the throne of grace and intercede for your family. Lead the prayers at the family altar and make sure the fire in the family altar never ceases. One habit that I have cultivated, by the grace of God, is

PRAY FOR YOUR FAMILY ALWAYS. STEP INTO THE THRONE OF GRACE AND INTERCEDE FOR YOUR FAMILY. LEAD THE PRAYERS AT THE FAMILY ALTAR AND MAKE SURE THE FIRE IN THE FAMILY ALTAR NEVER CEASES.

always praying for my family. It is lifting them up for God's protection and preservation upon their lives. No amount of money can compare to or would be a substitution for praying for your family. I often say that in most cases, when we pray, it seems like nothing is happening, but God is at work behind the scenes. My family and I have been in a car accident twice. Each time, the cars were wrecked, but thank God, none of those accidents injured us or took any of our lives. The first accident was revealed to me in a dream. I shared the dream with my wife and then asked for intercession as I lead in prayers. Later that day, someone ran into us at a stop sign, wrecking the car but not harming us. There is power in prayer, and we should be faithful in exercising this authority by always using it for our family, praying them into God's destiny.

Leading to Church

When men occupy the role of the priesthood, it eliminates the confusion witnessed in some homes where the man belongs to one church while the wife and the children belong to a different church. Most pastors are also not helping issues here because so many are seeking to grow the membership of their congregation. A man cannot sit at home watching sports or movies on a Sunday morning yet giving the order of which denomination he wants the family to attend. Sorry, sir, things do not work that way! This was the response I gave a young man who had a serious issue with the wife leaving their traditional denominational church to attend another. He told me his story about how hurtful it was that his wife made such a decision. As much as I sympathized with him, the fact remains that he had lost from the beginning. Our wives rarely will make such decisions if we take the lead of the priesthood in our homes. If men occupy the priesthood role, even when the wife feels the family should change the church, there will always be a mutual understanding. I once had a man ask me for counsel on his wife's decision for them to move to another church. First, I recognized his priesthood role because the wife did not make the decision alone; rather, she brought it to his attention for them to pray about. I told him that was a wonderful sign because she recognized his priesthood role. If he had not assumed and been functional in his priesthood role, the wife would have decided without consultation. I strongly advise that families attend the same church and that the man leads by waking up early Sunday morning to help get the entire family ready for the church service. That is how it ought to be and not the other way round. Do not make your wife be the one to wake the children and get ready for church. The man is the head and manages his house, especially on Sunday mornings.

> I STRONGLY ADVISE THAT FAMILIES ATTEND THE SAME CHURCH AND THAT THE MAN LEADS BY WAKING UP EARLY SUNDAY MORNING TO HELP GET THE ENTIRE FAMILY READY FOR THE CHURCH SERVICE. THAT IS HOW IT OUGHT TO BE AND NOT THE OTHER WAY ROUND.

Family Devotion

It is also the role of the man to ensure that daily family devotions occur as often as schedules will permit. In these present times, our work and school schedules are strained to the maximum. It is the responsibility of the man to make sure that the family regularly observes devotional time. Once such a foundational habit is formed, it will serve us well over lifetimes. The man should be the one to nurture and take the lead on this. Like I mentioned earlier, for a long time, I thought it was the norm for the woman to lead in this area. So, as I grew up, I did not bother to get myself involved in this aspect of the priesthood role at home. Thank God for the many wives who are leading and those who are assisting. Either way, God's grace is always upon our families. God's mercy is always upon us, but my principal point here is that when men carry out their priesthood role, it adds more strength to the family. Again, do not force the wives to chase you and the children for family devotion time. It does not work well that way. A family that prays together, stays together.

> IT IS THE RESPONSIBILITY OF THE MAN TO MAKE SURE THAT THE FAMILY REGULARLY OBSERVES DEVOTIONAL TIME. ONCE SUCH A FOUNDATIONAL HABIT IS FORMED, IT WILL SERVE US WELL OVER LIFETIMES.

Obedient to God's Word

We will discuss living out the life of priesthood in the next chapter, but I would like to emphasize that obedience is the key to answered prayers. Men ought not to allow anything to hinder their prayers.

Husbands, in the same way be considerate as you live with your wives, and treat them with respect as the weaker partner and as heirs with you of the gracious gift of life, so that nothing will hinder your prayers. (1 Pet. 3:7)

I will always encourage men not to waste time practicing priesthood in their homes if they are not ready to be obedient to God's word. The above verse from 1 Peter has renewed my mind for life. I do not want to waste my time. I want God to answer my prayers and according to His grace, He does. I have told my wife that it is no longer about how I feel whenever we have a misunderstanding but about how she (my wife) feels. That is my key concern. I cannot count how many times I have felt that I was right, but for peace to reign and for my prayers to be answered, I took the first step by apologizing. Why? The Bible says I should treat my wife with respect and that

THE HEAD WILL ALWAYS DO WHATEVER IT TAKES TO HAVE HIS FAMILY AT PEACE AND, ABOVE ALL, HAVING HEAVEN OPENED FOR ANSWERED PRAYERS.

settles it. As simple as this might sound, it is one of the troublesome issues in most families. I advise men not to wait for their wives to apologize first. If the wife is not forthcoming with an apology, be the first to offer it. Not every man will agree with me, and I respect the opinion of those who may have several issues about this book. However, I do not and never would want to just sound politically correct. I would rather say it as it is been placed on my heart and hope that I am contributing to the efforts of those whose intention is to reduce the statistics of homes with absent fathers. The head will always do whatever it takes to have his family at peace and, above all, having heaven opened for answered prayers.

Fathers, do not exasperate your children; instead, bring them up in the training and instruction of the Lord. (Eph. 6:4)

I once wrongly yelled at my son, and my wife called me to order about it. She explained to me in detail what had happened and her opinion on how I could have handled it rather than yelling. I not only saw reasoning from my

> **MY OBEDIENCE TO GOD'S WORD IS VERY VITAL IN MY HOME, AS IT IS FOR EVERY MAN WHO IS TO BE CONSIDERED THE HEAD OF THE FAMILY.**

wife's perspective, but I became very remorseful about my action. I swallowed my pride as a father and went straight to my son and apologized to him. Yes, I would rather obey God's word for an open heaven over my family. It is not about how I feel but how God is seeing me. A father apologizing to his child is, for me, a rare circumstance as I was born and raised in Africa, where such a thing would be considered taboo. I have no recollection of any time when my father apologized to me for taking an unjust action or making a wrong decision. I changed that tradition because I now know better, and I am an ambassador of Christ, building a kingdom-minded family. My obedience to God's word is very vital in my home, as it is for every man who is to be considered the head of the family.

Finally, just as it applies when dealing with our wives and children, so it is for every word of God. Intentionally obeying the word of God qualifies us into the priesthood.

If anyone turns a deaf ear to my instruction, even their prayers are detestable. (Prov. 28:9)

CHAPTER SIX

THE ROLE MODEL

In everything set them an example by doing what is good.
In your teaching show integrity, seriousness.
—Titus 2:7

I had a serious issue with my son, which made me realize he might benefit from having a mentor. I felt unqualified because I believed he would prefer someone able to relate to him as a friend, someone he would accept to coach and guide him. As a father, I got the shock of a lifetime when he gave me his response. He said, "Dad, I would rather that you mentor me than anyone else." It was a surprise to me since I have not always been perfect in dealing with him. It challenged me that if I wanted my son to look up to me as his mentor, then I must be an excellent role model for my family. Becoming an excellent role model is practicing the very word you teach and or preach. It is easy to teach about forgiveness until you find yourself in a situation that requires you to forgive. This is the very reason a man should get his life together. If you are teaching your kids about God's love and they are not seeing you show this love to their mom, you are confusing them. Many children grow up and walk away from God because the God we showed them at home makes little sense to them. The walk must match the talk.

I once met a man on a train, and an opportunity arose for us to chat. I asked if he was married and he said no, but he had children with his girlfriend. They both chose not to enter marriage because each of them had endured terrible experiences of a father who maltreated the wife. This man does not want to hurt the lady, and she does not want to be entangled in a marriage. They chose to remain unmarried so that if either feels they are tired of the relationship; they can amicably go their separate ways. Now imagine the role model their parents laid down for them and imagine what images they are passing down to their children.

> BECOMING AN EXCELLENT ROLE MODEL IS PRACTICING THE VERY WORD YOU TEACH AND OR PREACH. IT IS EASY TO TEACH ABOUT FORGIVENESS UNTIL YOU FIND YOURSELF IN A SITUATION THAT REQUIRES YOU TO FORGIVE. THIS IS THE VERY REASON A MAN SHOULD GET HIS LIFE TOGETHER. IF YOU ARE TEACHING YOUR KIDS ABOUT GOD'S LOVE AND THEY ARE NOT SEEING YOU SHOW THIS LOVE TO THEIR MOM, YOU ARE CONFUSING THEM.

What we read about priesthood can only make sense to our wives and children when they see us actively live out the life of priesthood. We do this not just because we want God to answer our prayers but because we want to pass down a wonderful legacy. Whatever life we live today has a great impact, either negatively or positively, on our family. Every man should strive to live a life of integrity. Children learn from what they see and not just what we tell them. If we teach our children the importance of prayers and they do not see us having our prayer time, all we say will never make sense to them.

> WHAT WE READ ABOUT PRIESTHOOD CAN ONLY MAKE SENSE TO OUR WIVES AND CHILDREN WHEN THEY SEE US ACTIVELY LIVE OUT THE LIFE OF PRIESTHOOD. WE DO THIS NOT JUST BECAUSE WE WANT GOD TO ANSWER OUR PRAYERS BUT BECAUSE WE WANT TO PASS DOWN A WONDERFUL LEGACY.

THE ROLE MODEL | 51

A good name is more desirable than great riches; to be esteemed is better than silver or gold. (Prov. 22:1)

I mentioned in the introductory part of this book how the integrity of my father affected my life positively when I had rebelled from the good upbringing I was given. Just the mention of my last name in my community gives my identity away. It tells you the standard of behavior expected of me, without words, because of the integrity associated with my parents and the family name. I need not say much to convince anyone to believe what I am saying because of the family I come from. In our community, my last name is associated with the traits of honesty and simplicity, so held in high esteem, which means a lot. This had a positive impact on me. I could not do or say anything without being concerned about messing up the integrity associated with my father's name. On the other hand, at the mention of some names, people would avoid contact, and other parents would forbid their children to associate with them. There are many people today with low self-esteem because of the shame their father brought to the family.

Men, just as the scripture in Proverbs 22:1 says, I chose to live a life that will honor my family rather than bringing shame to them. That is why we are to discuss those things that can jeopardize our integrity and how to overcome them. Hey, we are all a work in progress. I have seen no perfect man yet. But, let us choose integrity and lay down an excellent name for our families. Now, we will discuss those obstacles that ruin the lives of men and bring shame to the family.

> **I CHOSE TO LIVE A LIFE THAT WILL HONOR MY FAMILY RATHER THAN BRINGING SHAME TO THEM.**

Things That Ruin the Lives of Men
Sex

Flee from sexual immorality. All other sins a person commits are outside the body, but whoever sins sexually, sins against their own body.

Do you not know that your bodies are temples of the Holy Spirit, who is in you, whom you have received from God? You are not your own; you were bought at a price. Therefore honor God with your bodies. (1 Cor. 6:18–20)

The only option here is to flee from sexual immorality. Let every married man be faithful to his wife, and let the single man abstain from sex until he is married. I will not bore you with too many statistics here, but I will, in all honesty, share

> LET EVERY MARRIED MAN BE FAITHFUL TO HIS WIFE, AND LET THE SINGLE MAN ABSTAIN FROM SEX UNTIL HE IS MARRIED.

things that I know. Many men were in leadership positions but have lost their positions because of sexual immorality, some have contracted diseases that took their lives, and some took their own lives.

Pornography

In this new era of technology, the act of watching porn is destroying a lot of men in our society. Many men use pornography as an alternative in satisfying their sexual urge; some have even argued that there is nothing wrong with it. I would like to advise and speak out that there is everything wrong with it. Just as we are warned to flee from sexual immorality, please flee from porn. When Jesus addressed the question about committing adultery, hear what Jesus said for those arguing.

> You have heard that it was said, 'You shall not commit adultery.' But I tell you that anyone who looks at a woman lustfully has already committed adultery with her in his heart. If your right eye causes you to stumble, gouge it out and throw it away. It is better for you to lose one part of your body than for your whole body to be thrown into hell. And if your right hand causes you to stumble, cut it off and throw it away. It is better for you to lose one part of your body than for your whole body to go into hell." (Matt. 5:27–30)

If you have become involved with pornography, quickly flee from it and find a method of holding yourself accountable to stay away from it. Many cellular service companies and internet providers have a method to prevent such accessing problem websites. Do whatever you can to flee. Have your wife become your accountability person and take it to the Lord in prayers.

Love of Money

For the love of money is a root of all kinds of evil. Some people, eager for money, have wandered from the faith and pierced themselves with many griefs. (1 Tim. 6:10)

Many men are in jail today because of the love they have for money. Money is good. We all need money to survive on this planet earth. What I am saying is that many men's lives have been ruined by their love of money. The Bible says it is the root of all kinds of evil. It is the root of many of the atrocities being committed today. Drug trafficking, human trafficking, robbery, fraudulent businesses, internet hackers, and so forth. can be traced back to the love of money. Never accept an invitation or enticement from anyone to indulge in any illegal act of making money. You may make that money, but eventually, the scheme will backfire and come back to haunt you. Many kids today struggle because their fathers are somewhere serving a jail term because of the love for money. Let us focus only on legitimate means of making money, and it will come.

Alcoholic Drinks

Wine is a mocker and beer a brawler; whoever is led astray by them is not wise. (Prov. 20:1)

I titled my very first book, *Can I Take a Little Wine?* Although I have decided to publish a revised edition, I have never compromised from preaching total abstinence from consuming alcoholic drinks. Many of the negative events in life have some from the influence of alcohol.

In the Bible, Lot was lured into sleeping with his daughters because of the influence of alcohol. Some argue that we are to drink but not to excess. Many have also cited red wine as being healthy; however, all alcoholic drinks should be avoided if we are to be the role model. I tasted my first alcoholic drink at home. My dad drank alcohol but in moderation. When I began to drink, I could not keep my drinking in moderation. It almost ruined my life. God gave me a second chance. People say it is okay to drink moderately, but I ask, how much would be moderate? If athletes can discipline their drinking urge by avoiding alcoholic drinks, why can't I do the same? Some professions prohibit the drinking of alcohol while on duty. Men who wear the head of the family title should view the role as a profession that requires self-discipline and total abstinence from alcoholic drinks. Assume that you are at the airport, drinking alcohol in the little lounge area. The person beside you is also sipping an alcoholic drink. You suddenly realize that the person will be piloting your flight. What would be your immediate reaction? I might be misunderstood here, but I know that alcohol has done men more harm than good. As the head of the family, abstain from alcohol, desire to be in the right state of mind so you can hear God, see what He is showing you, and understand the vision.

> AS THE HEAD OF THE FAMILY, ABSTAIN FROM ALCOHOL, DESIRE TO BE IN THE RIGHT STATE OF MIND SO YOU CAN HEAR GOD, SEE WHAT HE IS SHOWING YOU, AND UNDERSTAND THE VISION.

And these also stagger from wine and reel from beer: Priests and prophets stagger from beer and are befuddled with wine; they reel from beer, they stagger when seeing visions, they stumble when rendering decisions. (Isa. 28:7)

Hard Drugs/Smoking

If you want to feel intoxicated, be filled with the Holy Spirit. Injecting or ingesting substances into your body or smoking makes little sense.

These vices are the acts of the devil and are taking a lot of lives today. We have many fathers on the street, homeless, because of the influence of drugs. Many cannot get a job today because their drug test always comes out positive. However, there is always a way out. Many organizations are embarking on helping with treatments and restoring men who have been substance abusers. I know of a young man who was captive to drug abuse. The church had done everything possible to help him but to no avail. During church service one Sunday, after several years of his absence from attending church, I saw the man but did not recognize him. I realized who he was when he shared his testimony on how he received treatment and was rescued by a Christian organization helping people with such addictions. Let us keep encouraging those who suffer from addiction about the importance of receiving treatment and above all, praying for them because the root cause of drug abuse is more spiritually rooted than physical.

> LET US KEEP ENCOURAGING THOSE WHO SUFFER FROM ADDICTION ABOUT THE IMPORTANCE OF RECEIVING TREATMENT AND ABOVE ALL, PRAYING FOR THEM BECAUSE THE ROOT CAUSE OF DRUG ABUSE IS MORE SPIRITUALLY ROOTED THAN PHYSICAL.

Anger

"In your anger do not sin": Do not let the sun go down while you are still angry and do not give the devil a foothold. (Eph. 4:26–27)

I called a friend of mine back home in Nigeria. He was very down and could not talk much. He promised to call back. When he called, I asked what the problem was. The story he told me was unbelievable, and yet, such stories are just a small glimpse of what anger has done to many men in our society. He told me about a young man who was a tenant of his, who had set his girlfriend ablaze with fire. The girl was so severely burned that by the time they arrived at the hospital, she was dead. While he was sharing this story with me, all I kept imagining in my head was, *what is it that can make a man so angry that he sets another human being on fire?* I can go on and on giving other examples of what anger is doing in the lives of men. I know that the story I shared is just one of many unimaginable stories caused by anger, but let me narrow it down to those minor issues which have wrecked homes. Most men are naturally inpatient, and whenever things are not going on as expected or imagined, they lose their temper. Again, I have learned my lesson here, and I have decided never to go to bed angry. No man knows what tomorrow will be. I encourage men to resolve issues as soon as possible. It is not worth it to delay resolving issues. When you stay comfortable in an angry mood, you are creating room for the devil. Most of the acts of atrocity being committed are fueled by anger.

> NO MAN KNOWS WHAT TOMORROW WILL BE. I ENCOURAGE MEN TO RESOLVE ISSUES AS SOON AS POSSIBLE. IT IS NOT WORTH IT TO DELAY RESOLVING ISSUES. WHEN YOU STAY COMFORTABLE IN AN ANGRY MOOD, YOU ARE CREATING ROOM FOR THE DEVIL. MOST OF THE ACTS OF ATROCITY BEING COMMITTED ARE FUELED BY ANGER.

Pride

> *Pride goes before destruction, a haughty spirit before a fall. Better to be lowly in spirit along with the oppressed than to share plunder with the proud.* (Prov. 16:18–19)

This is one act that ruins a lot of men. Because of my calling and passion for men, I have witnessed several times where it was obvious that help was needed, but the man will not allow such help because of pride. Many men will not read this book, and even if they read it, they will criticize and condemn it. I was invited to speak at a men's convention, and while on the stage pouring out my heart, encouraging the men who attended the conference, I noticed how one man kept staring at me. I felt he was not happy about what I was saying, and I was right.

He interrupted me with a question, and, by the grace of God, I politely gave him an immediate answer that the Holy Spirit gave to me and he became quiet. The conference became a life-changing experience for many, but I guess not for him. He was not happy because I rebuked a lot of men's wrong mentality toward women.

Setting a Good Example
Self-Control

Similarly, encourage the young men to be self-controlled. (Titus 2:6)

This is an important trait I teach my children, especially my first son. I need to live a self-controlled daily life myself so they will understand the meaning of the term. Although I am still a work in progress today, I am not where I used to be. I realized that when I control my temper, I am more effective in offering a correction. Learning self-control has helped me in parenting and bonding with my wife. When my son was little, I remember what my neighbor told me. He said I should enjoy my son now because once he becomes a teenager, it is a different game altogether. I could not understand that statement then, although we laughed over it. Today, I can assure you that it makes more sense to me. These days, I also try to avoid discussions that will lead to an argument with my wife while in front of the children. Such things matter a lot because the kids are sensitive in picking up on our nature. It also dawned on me to work on my temper when I saw my son mimicking me at a children's drama performed at a church concert. Again, everyone was laughing, but it was not funny for me. On our way back, I politely asked my wife if that personality was truly me, and she nodded yes. I decided not to pass

> I REALIZED THAT WHEN I CONTROL MY TEMPER, I AM MORE EFFECTIVE IN OFFERING A CORRECTION. LEARNING SELF-CONTROL HAS HELPED ME IN PARENTING AND BONDING WITH MY WIFE.

a fiery temper personality on to my children. I die daily to my flesh, so I can manifest a self-controlled life.

> **I DIE DAILY TO MY FLESH, SO I CAN MANIFEST A SELF-CONTROLLED LIFE.**

Honesty

The LORD detests lying lips, but he delights in people who are trustworthy. (Prov. 12:22)

The phone rang at home one day when I was so tired that I needed time for myself to rest. I ignored the phone, but I knew that my daughter was sitting close to me, and I knew that she would ask me why I did not pick up the phone. I told her I was too tired and that I would return the call once I felt rested. But that was not the truth. I had simply chosen to ignore the call. My daughter had asked me a question, but rather than telling her the truth, I covered up my dishonesty. I felt so bad that day, and yet I know that I have said things that are not true just to cover up in front of my kids. But I am not ashamed to tell the truth once I am convicted. Confessing only proves to our children that we are human.

Teachable

Fools find no pleasure in understanding but delight in airing their own opinions. (Prov. 18:2)

Just because I am a dad does not mean I should not be corrected. The more we accept correction when we are wrong, the better our kids learn to be teachable. While out on a drive one fateful day, I ate the last bit of my snack and then threw away the empty wrapper out onto the street. My daughter asked me

> **THE MORE WE ACCEPT CORRECTION WHEN WE ARE WRONG, THE BETTER OUR KIDS LEARN TO BE TEACHABLE.**

if I had thrown away the empty pack out on the street. I was so ashamed to admit my action, but I knew I had to live an honest life by saying the truth and I confessed. She then taught me about the undisciplined act I had displayed. I heard her, never covering up my error, and I promised to become better at being more disciplined.

Punctuality

But everything should be done in a fitting and orderly way. (1 Cor. 14:40)

If there is one great legacy that my dad passed down to me, I would say it is being punctual. My father is always on time and will always tell me to add time for uncertain incidents to any original time of estimate. I cannot remember him ever showing up for an appointment late. He is always on time and is well-known for that trait. When people made appointments with him, they would always be cautious of time because my father always kept on schedule. I strive to live such a life, praying that my children take up the legacy as they grow.

Giving

Do not withhold good from those to whom it is due, when it is in your power to act. Do not say to your neighbor, "Come back tomorrow and I'll give it to you"—when you already have it with you. (Prov. 3:27–28)

We are living in a generation filled with self-centeredness. Yet, I strive to teach and practice giving in front of my children. Investing in humanity is the greatest investment I can pass down to my children. I am a proud dad today because giving is becoming an essential part of their lives as well. We have a family slogan that is: God is blessing us to be a blessing.

Last Christmas, a friend told me how he and his family went to a shelter on Christmas

INVESTING IN HUMANITY IS THE GREATEST INVESTMENT I CAN PASS DOWN TO MY CHILDREN.

day to give of their time to serve the homeless. I was so inspired that I have already told my family that we will plan to go give of our time to serve others. It allowed me to share that giving is not limited only to money. Giving of time and talent is equally important.

Kindness

> David asked, "Is there anyone still left of the house of Saul to whom I can show kindness for Jonathan's sake?" Now there was a servant of Saul's household named Ziba. They summoned him to appear before David, and the king said to him, "Are you Ziba?" "At your service," he replied. The king asked, "Is there no one still alive from the house of Saul to whom I can show God's kindness?" Ziba answered the king, "There is still a son of Jonathan; he is lame in both feet." "Where is he?" the king asked. Ziba answered, "He is at the house of Makir son of Ammiel in Lo Debar." So King David had him brought from Lo Debar, from the house of Makir son of Ammiel. When Mephibosheth son of Jonathan, the son of Saul, came to David, he bowed down to pay him honor. David said, "Mephibosheth!" "At your service," he replied. "Don't be afraid," David said to him, "for I will surely show you kindness for the sake of your father Jonathan. I will restore to you all the land that belonged to your grandfather Saul, and you will always eat at my table." Mephibosheth bowed down and said, "What is your servant, that you should notice a dead dog like me?" Then the king summoned Ziba, Saul's steward, and said to him, "I have given your master's grandson everything that belonged to Saul and his family. You and your sons and your servants are to farm the land for him and bring in the crops, so that your master's grandson may be provided for. And Mephibosheth, grandson of your master, will always eat at my table." (Now Ziba had fifteen sons and twenty servants.) Then Ziba said to the king, "Your servant will do whatever my lord the king commands his servant to do." So Mephibosheth ate at David's[a] table like one of the king's sons. Mephibosheth had a young son named Mika, and all the members of Ziba's household were servants of Mephibosheth. And Mephibosheth lived in Jerusalem, because he always ate at the king's table; he was lame in both feet. (2 Sam. 9:1–13)

The scripture above is one of my favorites in the Bible. I encourage men to show kindness to their wives, children, and their neighbors. A little kindness shown to people makes an enormous difference in their lives. I pray that men will cultivate the heart that David showed to Jonathan's son by showing kindness and passing such a legacy on to their family and neighbors. Together we can reduce the statistics of absent fathers at homes. I cannot imagine a woman who would not willingly submit to a kind man for the rest of her life.

> I ENCOURAGE MEN TO SHOW KINDNESS TO THEIR WIVES, CHILDREN, AND THEIR NEIGHBORS. A LITTLE KINDNESS SHOWN TO PEOPLE MAKES AN ENORMOUS DIFFERENCE IN THEIR LIVES.

CHAPTER SEVEN
FEAR OF GOD

The fear of the LORD is the beginning of wisdom,
and knowledge of the Holy One is understanding.
—Proverbs 9:10

Every topic that is discussed in this book so far requires only one thing to be put into practice, the fear of God. We might read excellent books addressing issues about real men. We can listen to many messages, but when we fail to apply them in actual life, all knowledge or awareness gained just becomes a waste. It is time for every man who desires to make a change or a difference to reflect on what will happen to the soul after departing this planet earth.

In the early stages of my marriage, at times, I verbally abused my wife. Those times were like hell. Although I considered myself very spiritual, I lacked the wisdom of self-control. I allowed every little thing to cause me to lose my temper, and before I could control it, I would yell at the top of my voice. I believe that I was able to get away with this because my wife is an introvert. She never once challenged me when I shouted at her. However, every word that came out from my mouth emotionally destroyed her. She still cries whenever she remembers what I said to her back then.

Looking back now that I know better, I feel so ashamed of myself. But I thank God who allowed me, through a dream, to understand the consequences of the life I lived then. Whenever I share this dream, I always get goose bumps. In that dream, I saw everyone moving into a beautiful gate. As they moved, I could see the joy on their faces. Everyone entered the beautiful gate except me. I became worried and started questioning the man at the gate why I had not been called. He said my name was not on the list. I screamed and started recounting the many things I had done in the ministry and all the good deeds that I remembered. And yet, the man at the gate said to me, "Sorry, but your name is not listed." Again, I asked why, and immediately I saw a picture of me yelling at my wife and I heard all the offensive words I had used. I tried to explain what had happened, but I immediately woke up. I did not need a prophet to explain to me that if I had not woken up at that time, I would not have gone to heaven. I later recalled how upset I was with my wife the day before I had that dream.

When I asked the Holy Spirit to help me overcome such a horrible attitude toward my wife, it led me to realize that I was oppressing my wife. I thought, *what if she had walked away from our marriage because of my behavior?* Thank God she had not because I would have contributed to the increasing number of homes with absent fathers. Many wives and mothers have walked away from men who verbally abused them. Many men do not get the second chance that I enjoy today. I believe that is the primary reason I am writing this book. This chapter unveils the oppression men often use on their wives and how it has emotionally killed many women and is a contributing factor to the increase in divorce rates. While divorce is significantly increasing among Christians, you can only imagine what is happening in the secular world. Please understand that I was already a born-again Christian when I married my wife. I considered myself very spiritual, even though I was verbally abusing my wife. If the fear of God had not corrected me after the dream I had, I might still live in darkness and probably would have lost my marriage.

A lot of men have oppressed and are still oppressing their wives and kids, some unknowingly. The truth remains that there is always a final day of judgment. However, before that day, the truth we know will set us free. I am free today and want to free other men as well.

We will answer on the day of judgment for every action we take today. You can be passionate about the Lord, but without the fear of God, your life does not differ from a man who does not even know God. Now, let's discuss some oppressive behaviors that had led to so many divorces.

YOU CAN BE PASSIONATE ABOUT THE LORD, BUT WITHOUT THE FEAR OF GOD, YOUR LIFE DOES NOT DIFFER FROM A MAN WHO DOES NOT EVEN KNOW GOD.

Oppression

Do not take advantage of each other, but fear your God. I am the LORD your God. (Lev. 25:17)

Physical Abuse

Many men today physically abuse their wives. This is not right and should not be tolerated. Taking advantage of masculine strength to suppress your wife is the only circumstance where I encourage separation. It is very unfortunate that, even within the Christian community, we still have cases where dedicated and active churchmen physically abuse their wives in their homes. We must refrain from engaging in this destructive behavior. If you have done this in the past and have repented for doing so, I assure you that God has forgiven you. We must not dwell in the past and refuse to forgive ourselves. I do not mean this section to judge anyone but to teach that physical abuse is wrong. In certain circumstances, we may consider the first act an error, but subsequent ones are no longer innocent errors in judgment; they become intentional.

Verbal Abuse

Most everyone has been a victim of verbal abuse but that does not mean it is proper or acceptable. We must not verbally abuse our wives or children. Words carry considerable power and if not used properly, they will have a negative impact, especially on our children. If, while being upset, you begin cursing your child, telling him he is stupid and knows nothing, that child will grow up believing that he is so stupid and knows nothing. Children believe what their parents tell them. It compounds the error when your children use this learned behavior with their children.

Sexual Abuse

Sexual abuse happens in homes but, unfortunately, no one wants to address it. It is among the top reasons many women have walked away from their marriages. A man can be married, yet sexually abuse his wife. I have heard of incidents and complaints of men coming home late, drunk, and demanding sex with their wives. If the woman is not willing, the man overpowers her and forcefully has his way. Some men do not emotionally arouse their wives before demanding sex. This often irritates the wife, and when she does not cooperate, the man overpowers her. This also happens when women are in a particular stage of their menstrual cycle. Some women shy away from sex because of chemical body reactions, and yet, the man may force sexual intercourse against her wishes. I could go on and on with different examples of sexual abuse between married couples. The point I am stressing here is that such acts have led to many cases of women feeling violated because men felt it was their right and their wife's obligation to have sex when the man wants. This is not correct, and I strongly advise men to approach their wives with sensitivity and have full consent before engaging in sex. Never force sexual intercourse.

The fear of God is the best catalyst to checkmate certain actions men take. We now hear of fathers raping their daughters. I heard a terrible story that somewhere in Africa, the villagers discovered that a man was forcefully impregnating his daughter and selling the babies to human traffickers. What an abomination! Thank God the community found out and exposed the evil deeds this man has been involved with. When I hear such stories, I must ask, "Where is the fear of God?" and, "What is happening to this world?"

Unavailability

Some men, knowingly or unknowingly, avoid their family responsibilities. This puts a lot of pressure on the women to take charge of the home, including caring for the children. This lack of responsibility has caused or contributed to many divorces. One of my mentors shared with me what caused him the loss of his family. He frequently traveled away from home on business and in pursuit of making money. One day, upon his return from one of such trips, he arrived at an empty home. His wife and three children had left the home, and he could not comprehend what had happened. When he went over to their neighbor's home to inquire, he was told his family had moved to a different city. He was shocked and wondered why they had left him alone, without his prior knowledge that it was going to happen. He made further efforts to find them and was finally able to locate them. With the help of friends, he approached the wife to find out what caused her to take such a drastic decision. It filled the wife with sorrow as she expressed the pain and pressure the man's frequent travels had caused her and how her husband would not listen or try to understand things from her perspective. Thank God that marriage was able to be saved after the man rendered a genuine apology to his wife. My mentor then sternly warned me about making such an error in my marriage. Many homes have fallen apart because of the physical and emotional unavailability of the husbands at home.

MANY HOMES HAVE FALLEN APART BECAUSE OF THE PHYSICAL AND EMOTIONAL UNAVAILABILITY OF THE HUSBANDS AT HOME.

Not Providing

A wife who earns more than the husband should not be made to be responsible for paying all the household bills while the husband remains idle, not even giving non-financial support. There are instances of homes where the man makes the most money yet refuses to provide or contribute to the upkeep of the home.

This has caused misunderstandings among married couples and sometimes has led to divorces. In the previous chapter, we learned that the original intention of our Creator was that the woman was to be the helper. Therefore, in a home where the man does nothing, the woman will have nothing

> WE LEARNED THAT THE ORIGINAL INTENTION OF OUR CREATOR WAS THAT THE WOMAN WAS TO BE THE HELPER. THEREFORE, IN A HOME WHERE THE MAN DOES NOTHING, THE WOMAN WILL HAVE NOTHING TO HELP HIM WITH.

to help him with. I know of a woman who said the reason she remained a single mother was that it made no sense to live with a man who would not provide or support her at home. Single parenthood to her is not a big deal because she has paid for her home and takes care of all the bills without a man's support. Without a man's support, she feels there is no need for the man, and it is better to stay single than to be married. I get very emotional when addressing this issue. If men understood the harmful impact on the family, and especially on the children, their lack of provision and support causes, they would repent and assume the role of the family head. A man should count himself privileged if the wife is earning income and should not see it as an opportunity or excuse for him not to work, or working but using the money earned for other things that do not relate to family needs and expenses.

Tradition

Some women have suffered greatly because of certain customs or traditions that have allowed men to abuse their wives in the past. I am aware of those, especially the African immigrants, who came to the United States and then marry. Their marriages often fall apart because the man refuses to help the wife do domestic household duties. The women in many instances work eight to ten hours a day, and yet the man comes home, expecting his wife to cook, serve him food, and clean up after him, just because that is the way he thought or was taught, it should be. This tradition is against the original intent of our creator and has caused great harm in our marriages. Our wives are to help us run the home, and we should help them with the work at home, just as we do in our workplace. Men should make life easier for their wives and children. Our mandate is to do everything we can do to maintain a stress-free home for our family.

> OUR WIVES ARE TO HELP US RUN THE HOME, AND WE SHOULD HELP THEM WITH THE WORK AT HOME, JUST AS WE DO IN OUR WORKPLACE. MEN SHOULD MAKE LIFE EASIER FOR THEIR WIVES AND CHILDREN. OUR MANDATE IS TO DO EVERYTHING WE CAN DO TO MAINTAIN A STRESS-FREE HOME FOR OUR FAMILY.

Forceful Habits

There are instances of homes where the wives are coerced by their husbands into forming habits that have ruined them. Such destructive habits include drug abuse, alcohol abuse, smoking, and pornography, to mention but a few. There was a story a pastor once shared about a man who forced the wife to watch pornography with him. The woman refused because she understands the demonic influence attached to that act. This man kept pressuring her to watch pornography. The wife walked away from the marriage, taking their children with her. Men should cultivate the fear of God in order to live right and help their wives live right.

Leisure Time Abuse

This is another common area that causes men to mistreat women in their homes. I am not preaching against anyone who enjoys their leisure time. However, when the time devoted to watching sports, news, playing golf, or hanging out with buddies consumes time that is better invested in your wife or children, it becomes oppression. Men can become addicted to watching televised sports, especially when there is a tournament. This often causes them to be neglectful of what goes on around their home. Men are often addicted to playing golf or other sports that take their passion outside of their homes. When this continues, the woman at home feels lonely and has negative thoughts—of walking away from the marriage, or of trying to fill the void. I know of a woman that complains bitterly about how her husband, instead of coming home after work, goes to meet with his friends and then comes home late at night drunk.

> MEN ARE OFTEN ADDICTED TO PLAYING GOLF OR OTHER SPORTS THAT TAKE THEIR PASSION OUTSIDE OF THEIR HOMES. WHEN THIS CONTINUES, THE WOMAN AT HOME FEELS LONELY AND HAS NEGATIVE THOUGHTS—OF WALKING AWAY FROM THE MARRIAGE, OR OF TRYING TO FILL THE VOID.

Reversal of Roles

When a man loses his vision as the head of the family, a reversal of roles becomes inevitable. During a counseling session, I conducted, the man and the wife sat with me as we tried to resolve a few issues they had in their marriage. I listened as the woman lamented about how the man has failed in his role as the head of the family. She felt the husband relegates the lead to her, and she does not feel comfortable in that role. She continued, asking me if it is proper that she directs all the affairs of the home while the husband does nothing but follow. I transferred the question to the man. His response shocked me and showed that the woman was right in what she had said. This man believed that the wife should lead, and he would follow. He said that he felt his wife wanted to lead. I corrected his misconception and reminded him of his role as the head of his family. I told him it was apparent that the reason he was not filling that role was that he was not leading his family. When a woman sees the man fulfilling his role in his family, she follows to help, but the reverse is the case when a man loses his vision. I told him that his decision was causing more harm. I referred

> WHEN A MAN LOSES HIS VISION AS THE HEAD OF THE FAMILY, A REVERSAL OF ROLES BECOMES INEVITABLE.

him back to the blueprint which we discussed in chapter three. I instructed him that God made him the head, not by choice, but by mandate. I told him that his wife was there to help and not to lead. I challenged him and, praise God, he stood up and took the lead. Today, that family stands firm and united, still happily married. The Creator designated the man to lead his family, and the wife is to help and support her man to accomplish God's purpose concerning their family.

> **THE CREATOR DESIGNATED THE MAN TO LEAD HIS FAMILY, AND THE WIFE IS TO HELP AND SUPPORT HER MAN TO ACCOMPLISH GOD'S PURPOSE CONCERNING THEIR FAMILY.**

CHAPTER EIGHT
IMPACT OF FATHERLESSNESS

But you, God, see the trouble of the afflicted;
you consider their grief and take it in hand.
The victims commit themselves to you; you are the helper of the fatherless.
—Psalm 10:14

After my dad lost his father when he was only nine years old, life became miserable for him and his three siblings. The family depended on him because he was the oldest of the four kids left behind with their mom. The death of my grandfather happened during the 1930s. At that time, it was customary for a brother of a deceased married male to take the widow in levirate marriage. This was the case with my grandmother; her brother-in-law was now to become her husband. She detested the idea and made the brave decision to run away with her children, leaving behind everything she had accumulated with her late husband. They were considered wealthy, as my grandfather was one of the very few men with a higher level of formal education and he worked with the State Ports Authority. My grandmother's decision cost her their home, financial resources, and the "death in service benefit" she received when her husband died. Because a decision not to submit to the levirate marriage was considered taboo, no one would assist her. She had to work extremely hard to make ends meet, beginning with petty trading and learning to stitch fabrics using a hand-held sewing machine. According to my dad, Grandma had set aside most of the money she earned so he could acquire a formal education up to the highest level achievable. My dad, while still in school, took a part-time job because it was

THE ABSENCE OF A FATHER IN THE HOME HARMED MY DAD AND HIS SIBLINGS IN SO MANY WAYS, BUT GOD SAW THEM THROUGH.

not financially easy for the family. Please remember that my dad was only nine when he lost his father. His family had enjoyed the presence of the father and the comfort that came with his wealth. And then, in a wink of an eye, their lives turned upside down. My dad could spend a lifetime narrating their ordeal, especially what life threw at his mom.

The absence of a father in the home harmed my dad and his siblings in so many ways, but God saw them through. My grandmother committed them into the hands of the Lord and made every effort to train them to follow in the path of the Lord. Everything turned out well for them, and today it has become just history. My grandmother and her children never gave up. After my dad graduated from school and gained full-paid employment, he started contributing toward the upbringing of his younger siblings, two brothers and one sister. His sister married a police officer and raised successful kids. His younger brother became a successful business entrepreneur, and his youngest brother became a medical doctor. As for my dad, he earned his master's degree and is employed as a textile engineer in Lowell, Massachusetts.

The negative impact on them after losing their father and the family head does not compare to the later glory of their lives. Grandma lived a full life, dying at a hundred and two years of age. As I write this book, my father is still alive at ninety-eight years. Despite all the ordeals that surrounded his growing up, he successfully fulfilled his fatherly role for me and my siblings. He continues to do the same today for members of his community.

Any time Dad tells his family's life history, I hear how God saw them through all their struggles and challenges. God filled the vacuum created by the loss of their father and family head.

It always blessed me to hear my grandma's version of it all while she was still alive. She enjoyed having her grandchildren around her when she told the family stories. She never complained or expressed remorse for her decision and its consequences. Grandma always committed all to God and became even more strongly devoted to her Christian life. Her story reminds me of the scripture, Psalm 68:5: "A father to the fatherless, a defender of widows, is God in his holy dwelling." God defended my grandma, strengthened her, and encouraged her throughout her life journey. The Lord is indeed the father of the fatherless.

Some people experience the absence of their father, not because he passed away, but for various other reasons. Most times, their father just walked away from the family.

My purpose in writing this chapter is to encourage everyone who is a member of a family where the family head is absent. Do not allow the present situation or circumstances to determine your future. Destiny is in the hands of God. The absence of

DO NOT ALLOW THE PRESENT SITUATION OR CIRCUMSTANCES TO DETERMINE YOUR FUTURE. DESTINY IS IN THE HANDS OF GOD. THE ABSENCE OF A FATHER CAN HARM LIVES.

a father can harm lives. We cannot deny knowing that the resulting vacuum is filled when we trust in the Lord—it makes a tremendous difference. Never live your life dependent on having your father present. A loved one can be suddenly absent because of death and the other reasons I have explained. You have a heavenly Father whose nature cannot be compared to the absent dad. Jesus is the dad every one of us needs. His love is unconditional, His mercies endure forever, and His grace suffices to see you through. The best way to move forward is to read and listen to stories of successful people who have been in the same or similar situation. Keep encouraging yourself that your own life can be meaningful and fruitful regardless of life's trials and setbacks.

A boy grew up without his biological father, but God saw him through, and he grew up to become President of the United States of America. Freddie Figgers was a baby abandoned in a dumpster, but today he is a multi-millionaire with several companies of his own. I could go on and on to telling how God has been and still is a Father to the fatherless.

Let me conclude this chapter by sharing with you the testimonies of two personal friends of mine, who are doing amazing work in our community today. The first contributor is a friend, brother in Christ, and my personal banker. He also fellowships with us at Men of Faith Network. The second testimony is from another friend, who is also a brother in Christ. He serves with me on the board of trustees at Men of Faith Network.

> NEVER LIVE YOUR LIFE DEPENDENT ON HAVING YOUR FATHER PRESENT. A LOVED ONE CAN BE SUDDENLY ABSENT BECAUSE OF DEATH AND THE OTHER REASONS I HAVE EXPLAINED. YOU HAVE A HEAVENLY FATHER WHOSE NATURE CANNOT BE COMPARED TO THE ABSENT DAD. JESUS IS THE DAD EVERY ONE OF US NEEDS. HIS LOVE IS UNCONDITIONAL, HIS MERCIES ENDURE FOREVER, AND HIS GRACE SUFFICES TO SEE YOU THROUGH.

Despite those miserable times in their lives when they experienced the absence of their fathers in their lives, God saw them through. They stayed focused, believed in God, and truly it came to pass they did not end up on the wrong side of life. I encourage anyone in similar circumstances to renew your faith and believe that God is your Father. There are no more excuses for a life that does not have a positive influence on the people around you. Please know that your decision today will greatly affect your future. Now, read true-life stories of these two exceptional men of God.

Longe S.—A Brief Life Story

I was born in Zaire, Central Africa, known now as the Democratic Republic of the Congo. My father worked for the government overseas, and because of the political unrest, he moved the family to the United States. My parents divorced before I was born and neither one had established faith in Jesus Christ. My dad remarried, and when we came to this country, we settled in the town of Wauwatosa, Wisconsin.

Living with my stepmom and dad was difficult. I felt constantly abused and under-appreciated by my stepmom. My dad was nowhere to be found when I needed him. I was thirteen years old when I came to this country. For all the time I spent at home, it felt as if my stepmom never wanted me or my brothers, preferring her biological children over us. She constantly degraded and ridiculed me and my siblings for almost every action. There was never any recognition for doing something positive, but she always criticized anything negative. My memories of my dad before he remarried were great and peaceful, and he was very involved in our lives. I even recall him carrying me on his shoulder after playing soccer with him. Back then, I felt the love and saw how much he cared for me and my brothers. He was there when we needed him.

I saw a turning point after he remarried and a few months after arriving in America when we began living with my stepmom. It felt as if my dad did not care or had simply decided to neglect his responsibilities as a father. My dad is well-educated with a doctoral degree, but when it came to family, he literally blew it and failed miserably. His wife abused my brothers and me, and he never came to our rescue or made an effort to do anything about it, especially when it was very obvious. When I started high school, my dad was not involved in my education, aside from the basic requirements needing his response so he would not look bad in front of the principal and teachers.

The reason I decided to move forward with my story is the hope that it may bless someone else and shed light on having an absent dad or a dad who remarried but was not involved in their children's lives.

Growing up and living with my dad and stepmom is an experience that I would not wish even for my worst enemies. Looking back now, I recognize how she abused me. My dad was not there to help, and he would often take my stepmom's side. How lonely life felt when I had a father who simply did not want me and seemed not to care, allowing bad things to happen to me. He only tried to keep an image of a loving father for others, so as to not to be judged or be looked badly upon. Ironically, he would take us to church, but looking back now, I think the desire was not pure. At home, I felt lonely, isolated, and tolerated only because I was not yet eighteen years old. I look at my high school experience and do not recall a time when he came to support me or encourage me. All his attentions were spent on my stepmom and her children. It makes me wonder where my life would have been if I had the kind of support that is every child's desire growing up.

As many of my peers were looking forward to college and enjoying their high school years, I spent most of my time wondering what life would be like if I had the proper home and a dad who desired the best for me and my future. I would spend many nights going to bed crying because I felt unloved and distant from my dad. He allowed my stepmom to treat me and my siblings the way she saw fit with no accountability, allowing her to put her children's needs and desires above ours. The only time I felt any love was when they needed something from me or wanted me to babysit my stepbrothers and sister. Growing up, I hated my life and hated everything about myself. It was hard growing up in the mid-1990s as an African-American boy and not having the support at home. It made my life so much more undesirable in contrast to my white friends, who seemed to have a spotless life, parents who cared for them, and who wanted them to succeed. I honestly started to believe that my dad never cared about me or my plans for my future. He never asked, making me wonder why he brought us to America. Hence, it dawned on me one day that it was God's plan to bring us to America; otherwise, it did not make sense to live in a home where I felt neglected.

As I started my senior year in high school, my stepmom decided to visit the state of Vermont to see a friend or family member. She fell in love with the state and convinced my dad to move there with her and her children only. This was a spontaneous decision and a move that showed me that my dad did not have me in mind as being part of the plan. I saw my dad making decisions without even consulting me or asking my opinion on things that drastically affected me. I was never relevant to him; each of his decisions were made to benefit only my stepmom and her children.

A week or two before my high school graduation, I became homeless for almost forty-eight hours. Unbeknown to me, my dad had decided to relocate and join my stepmom, who had already moved to Vermont a few months prior. I knew what was coming after I graduated by reading between the lines. It made sense that once my stepmom finally moved there, it was only a matter of time before my dad would follow. What shocked me and left me unguarded was when my dad decided to leave before I graduated. He kicked me out of the house before leaving, not knowing where I was going to stay or whether I even had a place to go. He assumed that it would not be an issue for me because I am likable. But because they restricted me from hosting friends at home, I did not have a relationship with anyone to a point that I could stay at their home. Plus, I felt embarrassed and had no car use for travel. I knew that I needed to find a place immediately after graduation but never thought my dad would leave me before my big day with absolutely no warning or a heads-up that he was planning to do it that early. I had no place to go and no friend to come to my rescue. I had no clue what to do with my suitcases since I did not have a car or a job at the time. Only by God's grace was I able to convince one of our next-door neighbors to keep my belongings. They assumed that I had done something bad for my dad to leave me like that. They did not want to host me, either thinking I was going to stay there longer, or they did not want to take on the responsibility of a senior. Although they never said it, I knew that was what they were thinking. They agreed to keep my belongings until I was ready to pick them up.

I spent the day lingering at restaurants and cafes just to have a place to rest. At night, I rode buses from one end of the route to the other end as a way to keep myself warm until my oldest brother could pick me up and take me to his college dorm, where he lived at the time. During that time, I questioned God, wondering where he was, and why he allowed so much pain in my life. I asked why I didn't have a mom in my life and why my dad allowed me to be abused and neglected, especially as I was wrapping up my senior year without any concern about where I would end up. My pain was real and hard to swallow. My dad declared me his enemy without me ever knowing or being able to understand why he hated me and wanted nothing to do with me. I was not a perfect child, but I tried my best to please him. He never reciprocated my love, from my teenage years into my adulthood. My dad purposely missed my high school graduation, my graduation after two years of college, and my graduation after four years of college. He did not come to my wedding, even though he was invited after my brother and I went to Vermont to visit him and make peace.

I believe getting into alcohol and drugs would have been a justifiable excuse for me based on the pain I experienced and endured most of my life. Sometimes, I wonder if my life would have been better if my dad had been directly involved. As I reflect, I also see the hands of God protecting me and guiding me in those lonely and painful times. God saw my pain and sorrow and encouraged me to continue school and work hard to get to where I am now. Although my faith was not always as strong as it is now, I knew that God loved me, that Jesus Christ died for my sins, and that I did not come to this country to fail. Despite all the obstacles, He can get me through them. I did not have a Plan B or C, only Plan A, which was to rely on God to help me since my brother and I were struggling and had no other support. I say this humbly, but most times, I wanted to die and saw death as a better path to alleviate or end my pains. I did not feel needed by the world. Satan tried to use those pains to push me to commit suicide, but I thank God that I did not own a gun and wasn't living in a house with a garage during those painful times alone.

People look at me now and give credit to my parents, especially my dad, for how I turned out. I rarely correct them because of the painful memories. But when I do, I make sure to let them know that it is God who deserves all the glory for who I am. Christ is the reason I'm still alive and the very reason for all of my successes. I have learned through my pains that having Jesus with nothing equals everything, but having everything without Jesus equals

> CHRIST IS THE REASON I'M STILL ALIVE AND THE VERY REASON FOR ALL OF MY SUCCESSES. I HAVE LEARNED THROUGH MY PAINS THAT HAVING JESUS WITH NOTHING EQUALS EVERYTHING, BUT HAVING EVERYTHING WITHOUT JESUS EQUALS NOTHING.

nothing. I also learned that no matter the situation or the pain, Christ is in control, and He always has our best interest in mind. My advice is simple but can be hard to swallow; trust God and don't give up on him no matter what and, if you can, find a good church and let someone godly and trustworthy come by your side to pray for you and guide you through your pain because we were never meant to fight alone. Finally, do not allow Satan to point to God as the enemy.

Rob F.—Growing Up in a Single-Parent Household without Guidance, without Love—Its Impact on a Maturing Child

The following reflects some of my experiences and the impact of growing up in a one-parent home. It should be noted that I was without a full-time father, but I also believe having a missing mother would produce similar results. A single parent cannot be both a caregiver and disciplinarian, no matter the dedication and capabilities given the financial, organizational, and emotional needs of a family. Children suffer as they grow and develop. Many have low self-esteem, loneliness, belligerence, lack of trust, and have difficulty in relationships.

I am sharing my history to help parents understand that the consequences of splitting a family are manifested in their children and may produce behavioral aberrations that adversely affect their lives. Even if a person is powerless to do anything to stop the marital split, understanding that there are negative consequences gives one insight to keep a watchful eye out and address them as they occur.

There is no substitute for love to a child. Love builds trust and security. Love your children as God loves you! If your relationship cannot be saved, do not let your children pay for it. Work with the other parent for the common good of the children.

My story is that I grew up without a father living in the

> **THERE IS NO SUBSTITUTE FOR LOVE TO A CHILD. LOVE BUILDS TRUST AND SECURITY. LOVE YOUR CHILDREN AS GOD LOVES YOU! IF YOUR RELATIONSHIP CANNOT BE SAVED, DO NOT LET YOUR CHILDREN PAY FOR IT.**

home. My mom was a good mother who worked for many hours and did her best. I know she loved us, but she used us as weapons against our father. She ultimately drove him to leave our home and for the most part, our lives. My dad was driven to do some very desperate things to be in our lives. When I was a baby, my dad took me to Wisconsin and was subsequently arrested for kidnapping me. This was the early 1950s, and fortunately, the police came to the appropriate conclusion and dropped the charges after he gave my mother what she was looking for.

She continued her assaults on my dad and eventually drove him away. Although he had moved away, he had my sister and me every other weekend and spoke to us on the phone when our mother allowed. My mom spoke badly to us about him and told us untruths until he finally could take it no more and our visitations diminished until we became adults and could make our own decisions.

My mom set the bar low when it came to expectations in school. She took a path that was short on discipline and long on ease and had very little time to devote to us. If we got passing grades and avoided major trouble, she was satisfied, unlike my dad who wanted us to be all we could be. At one point, my dad wanted me to come to live with him. Unfortunately, my mom played on that to tell us that if we lived with our father, there would be no TV or fun. She told us many untrue things that affected our opinions toward our father and hurt him badly.

I grew up on the south side of Chicago during an exceedingly difficult time. I developed skills related to violence and roamed the streets with my friends. First, it was throwing rocks, then fist fighting, then knives, and finally the ultimate weapon at the time—a zip gun which we made with the help of the older guys.

When I was less than ten years of age, my friends—or maybe more accurately put, unnamed gang members and I traveled across the city to Rainbow Beach or Comiskey Park unaccompanied. The lack of time for supervision by my mother contributed to my "independence." While playing sports, I continually looked to see if my dad or my mom showed up, but neither was ever there.

I grew up starving for acceptance but never finding it as a youth. I became lonely, with low self-esteem, confused, not living up to my potential, and wandered from one fun time to another while living in a fog. As I look back on those days, I realized I had done things that I would never have allowed my children to do. I do not blame either of my parents but rather am simply stating the facts. I lived with nightmares that I would tell my mom about, and she would assure me that were only bad dreams, except they were not. I learned later in life that those nightmares were real.

Although we were raised with the church as part of our routine, religion was also left behind after my serving in the army.

I was a good person but without the love and discipline of a father, I became wayward and developed a pattern of living moment to moment seeking acceptance and fun. This caused me to be a slave to fun and acceptance. I did not develop the proper relationship morals and lived a life of sin. Because of what I endured, I vowed I would never have children and possibly have them live through what I had.

As I look back on my life, two things have defined my struggles, and the latter resulted from the former—no father in my house and God absent from my life.

I did love children. My nieces and nephews were my surrogate children. My nephew was four when I left for the army, and the morning I left, as I said goodbye, he hugged my legs and cried "Don't leave me, Uncle Hero." It was a difficult moment. At thirty-four, I became a father—by accident rather than design. With that reality, it overjoyed me to become a dad and swore I would be the best dad I could for my child.

With this, my moral compass evolved, and I quit living for the moment and dedicated myself to my child. Soon I had three, a son and two beautiful daughters. I had them baptized and started them in church but still struggled with my faith. I loved being a father! I loved my children with all my heart and soul and protected them and ensured they were raised with good values and expectations. Unfortunately, my wife went the way of my mother and more. One day I was served with divorce papers, and three days later her friend moved in. She used tactics remarkably similar to my mom's, but even worse at times.

As difficult and depressing as it was, I remembered my experiences without a dad, and I did my best to be there for my children, despite their mother. My children and I endured many rough times, but I stood my ground and was the father my children needed and I desired to be.

I WAS THERE! Having a loving father as a part of a person's life makes all the difference in the world how we develop and what we become.

I have a wonderful loving relationship with my children. My son is one of my best friends and still lives with me. It is not from need, as he is an attorney and a CPA. My oldest daughter has given me a sweet, beautiful granddaughter whom I adore. The icing on the cake is I found my faith and love God!

This is thanks in part to my brothers and friends at both Men of Faith Network and my church. I currently serve as a board member of the Men of Faith Network and as a hospitality minister. I belong to the Knights of Columbus at my church.

Postscript: After my dad died, my sister found a briefcase and brought it to me saying, "You better look in here and see and read what is in it." There was evidence of our father's love and how he struggled to keep his family. There was also the evidence that proved those nightmares were real and not just bad dreams. It should be noted that my sister also suffered many issues related to growing up without a father. Her life was difficult in similar but slightly different ways. She departed this earth at the young age of forty-nine.

But you will receive power when the Holy Spirit comes upon you, and you will be my witnesses in Jerusalem, throughout Judea and Samaria, and to the ends of the earth. (Acts 1:8)

CHAPTER NINE
TESTIMONY

These things happened to them as examples and
were written down as warnings for us,
on whom the culmination of the ages has come.
—1 Corinthians 10:11

Learn from Mistakes

After reading this far, I am sure you can see how deeply passionate I am about writing this book. It is not my intention that it be just another book placed on the bookshelf. I have consistently poured out all that is laid on my heart, and I have shared real-life scenarios to impact lives. This additional section retells true stories told by people I know personally. Their testimonies have been included so you can learn from other's mistakes and see how God has helped them through it all. Please, learn from the advice they have shared.

Jeffery T.—Chicago, IL

Writing about my journey to faith was a wonderful challenge. I want to thank Brother Fredrick, and the prodding of the Holy Spirit, for enabling me to tell my story. I am a husband, father, businessman, and a blood-born Jew. And yet, I am, first and foremost, a believer in Yeshua Messiah.

85

My faith journey has not been limited to the period from the day I accepted Jesus as savior through this moment in time. It started much earlier, as a boy who did not grow up in a faith-based home.

I was born to secular Jewish parents and raised in Skokie, Illinois, a suburb of Chicago, at a time when America was experiencing the greatest blessings and curses as a free nation. I did have exposure to the Bible in a "traditional style" synagogue where, as an eight-year-old boy, we began to learn to read and write (but not speak) the Hebrew language; I enjoyed learning this ancient and strange writing. It seemed odd to me that we did not go as far as learning to speak the language. I later understood that with only ninety minutes per day, three times per week, the rabbis and teachers had limited time to prepare us to pray in Hebrew. A young boy is trained up to prepare for the Bar Mitzvah at the age of thirteen. This is when the journey to be a man begins according to the traditions and teachings of the Jewish religion. It is the date marker where the responsibility of being a Jewish male begins and should grow throughout life. We were being prepared to sing, chant, and pray out loud from the Torah, the five books of Moses, and other Jewish traditional works.

During early adulthood, I had little exposure to the God of Abraham, Isaac, and Jacob, much less Jesus, except an occasional service at a house of faith for a wedding or a funeral. The truth that the "wages of sin is death," was not even a fleeting thought in those years. However, I was fortunate enough to have a good work ethic, and so I embarked on my career path to becoming a commercial photographer. The work was mostly for ads, magazines, and catalogs. I loved the work, and it was my dream come true as far as a career.

In 1980, I was working at a large photo studio in Chicago, I met my first wife-to-be when I was twenty-three and she was eighteen. She had just graduated high school. She was also not raised with faith in Christ. We fell for each other and moved in with each other six months after meeting. No marriage, no commitment, and living in sin. For me, I did not even have the slightest thought that what we were doing was sinful. We loved each other, and that was enough, or at least so I thought. One day, she missed her period and without hesitation, we went to the abortion clinic to do the worst thing we could do. Thoughts of how wrong and evil this was had not even come into our minds. We simply made the appointment. They did a final pregnancy test before we scheduled the abortion and praise God, we were *not* pregnant. I remember being so relieved. Looking back, I believe that God was merciful, so very gracious, and so we did not have to experience a terrible and sinful abortion.

To all my brothers in Christ—trust in the Lord first, and put away your flesh temptations. Be sure you seek the counsel of wise and Godly men in all you do. I realize that when we are young, we feel like we are invincible, but we are nothing without the grace and mercy of God through the sacrifice of Jesus our Lord. *Please* read Proverbs every day. There are thirty-one proverbs, one for each day of the month. Read them for a month and then start over the next month. Do this without fail, and the wisdom of God will become part of your life.

In 1984, we got married after living together for three years. Still, our lives had no exposure to Jesus or a Godly life. We both worked, partied, smoked some marijuana, and even did some cocaine now and then, as well as drinking alcohol regularly. None of these is any kind of excuse, but worthy of mention as we lived the "typical" secular lifestyle. My first son came along in 1989 and my second son in 1993. We raised them as good boys, but without any God-based principles, Bible, or religion. Throughout our marriage, we were good friends but never seemed to be in love, and without God, the marriage started to crumble. First, we separated, but since we owned a home together, we lived separated in the same home. We both dated much too soon, while we were still sharing a home. I had relations with many other women during this period, and she had men as well. Eventually, anger, bitterness, and resentment, along with no foundation of worth, including many sinful natures, started seeping in. We eventually divorced in 1996. The only saving grace was that we remained friends. It was hurtful to my young boys, but because I lived close to them and we had joint custody, the boys did not feel quite as devastated, especially after some time had passed.

To all my brothers in Christ—take heed from my mistakes, listen, and learn that you do not have to go through the grief of divorce. God hates divorce, and He loves you. He knows your future wife. Pray for your future wife (or your current wife) every day without ceasing. Ask the Lord to protect your heart and to make you the Godly man that He has chosen you to be for your wife. When problems arise, do not let the sun go down on your anger. Seek reconciliation always and quickly! The purpose God has is for you and your wife to become one flesh.

I met my second wife in this period, and we had a fling before we got married. I do not know why I married her because I did not love her, but I enjoyed her company. At this time, I started to get signals which I now know was the prompting of the Holy Spirit. She and I were married in Mexico on the beach by a priest. I was not even Catholic. This marriage lasted two years, and it was during this time that I came to faith in Christ. She kept her Catholic traditions. She had altars with candles in the house, which I found to be concerning. I tried as a young Christian to save the marriage, but it just was not happening, and she was convinced that I had an affair. This was not true, but I did not argue. We just divorced.

To all my brothers in Christ, healing must take place in life before we are ready to live a new life in Christ after terrible events. I did not do that and rushed into getting married again. Yes, I was not yet saved, but please learn that brokenness is not something to be taken lightly. Do not rush; do not go out of the will of the Lord. If you have children, they are the most important people during your single period. (God is *always* Number One, and then your wife.)

All along these broken roads, I shared the responsibility of raising my boys according to a custody arrangement. My first wife had moved to California with my boys. I could have fought against it, but I did not, and I allowed them to move far away. Later, the boys would come live with me, which was something they wanted to do since I was always doing my best to care for them.

To all my brothers in Christ, stay close to your children. Raise them with the Lord and by sharing the Bible.

Then I met my third wife. I was still a baby Christian, and she was also a Christian. I felt as if this would be it, and I dedicated myself to a good marriage. I have, like all sinners, many flaws, and getting back to financial responsibility was my struggle. I had issues with hating myself for past sins and for the pain I had caused myself and others. My boys were still growing strong and healthy, praise God, and they moved back to California to attend college. My wife had a daughter who at first seemed to like me, but immediately after the wedding, she went into a downward spiral and started to hate me. We worked on these issues with counselors that, on the surface, seemed to have a Christian world-view, but they seemed less interested in praying and more in clinical ways to start a healing process. My ex-daughter-in-law had issues of abandonment because her father had left her without saying good-bye. Sad as it is, I became the scapegoat. I understood this, and I tried to be as gentle as possible, giving her plenty of space. She was passive-aggressive and would not let go of the bitter hatred. This put tremendous pressure on the marriage, and it chipped away at the love my wife had for me to the point of her regretting that she married me. I was devastated. I thought, *We are both Christian, so we can commit to God and work this out.* But my wife's heart was hardened and she refused. I initially refused to divorce her because there appeared to be no grounds in the Bible for this. After much counseling, pain, tears, and confusion, it was explained to me that the hardening of the heart can be a reason for divorce. I had done everything I could in prayer, and it was still allowed. This was the worst time of my life. The day I moved out, her mother was there watching me, and it felt like I was a criminal. Her daughter wrote me a scathing painful and awful letter, which took a long time to recover from after reading. I eventually, forgave all of them, and finally had to go into a deep meltdown with God to fully heal.

To all my brothers in Christ—Fight for your marriage, change, pray, fast, and try to take a "cooling off period" before making any rash decisions. I did not have an opportunity to request a separation period as she would not accept this option. But we as men *must* fight for this at all costs. Please do not give up. Fight for your marriage.

Soon, the enemy got to me, and I was not strong. I desired female companionship, and so I dated even before the divorce was final. What was I thinking? I knew the Word, yet I fell and because I let loneliness and despair take the place of Jesus, I became like a lost man and sinned with women and turned from the Lord.

To all my brothers in Christ, Proverbs 5:3–9 tells you what to do. I did not heed these holy words, and therefore, God would soon break me down again.

During my period of recovery, the "enemy" sifted me and tried to destroy me completely. He lied to me every day, putting demonic voices in my head that said, "See, your Christianity has done nothing but cause you pain and everyone you love has abandoned you." By the grace of God, I knew this was a lie from the pit of hell, but when I was so weak, it was difficult not to hear this message and not be afflicted. The enemy also caused me to go broke, but God allowed this to happen. I have blame in this as well, as I was so depressed that I could hardly get out of bed. Yet, I worked my small business and got a job, doing both to survive. Still, the money was limited, and at one point I had zero money, no paycheck, and no gas to go to my work. I curled up in a fetal position in bed late one night, and I cried out to God, "I am finished. I cannot take any more." With my tears still streaming, I somehow fell asleep. When I awoke the next morning, the sun was shining, the birds were gently singing, and I slowly rose and made a cup of coffee. It felt different, vastly different. I sat there in a chair listening to God's creation, and a peace came over me that surpasses all understanding. God had heard my prayers—*all* of them. This peace was the last time I had any doubt that God had written me into the Lamb's Book of Life. I was on my way, with Jesus, to being completely healed. Praise the Lord,; His steadfast love endures forever!

I pulled back and stopped dating, I repented, and I asked God to renew me once again. I started attending church again and reading the Word. I had put my profile on a dating site called Christian Mingle for a time, but I pulled off. One day, I got a response from a nice lady who asked why I did not respond to her. I was compelled to at least answer, so I pulled out my credit card and signed back up. Once we connected, I felt it may be worth one more attempt to find a Christian woman and so, carefully, I continued to talk.

I met my wife, love, and partner, on February 23, 2014, at a neutral spot in Chicago. We had already been talking for two weeks and knew we were both solid believers. I was honest with her from the start about everything. She also came from a broken past. I had two grown adult sons who were not yet married, and she had three daughters, including one set of identical twins, all married, and seven grandchildren. The odd thing was, she and I attended her parents' church the very next day. We knew we were friends from the start. That is very unusual. I look back and think about how bold, and a bit crazy, it was that we would attend church the day after we met. But it was a sweet and wonderful experience.

We dated every week and saw each other a lot, including going to church together every week. She was caring for her aging mom and staying at her parents' house. To make this more complex, her father was the pastor of the church that we attended. His belief is that divorced men and women should not date as he did not believe in remarriage. We respected his beliefs completely, and I would not enter the house as a guest until we were married. We had no problem whatsoever with this arrangement. We stayed pure until marriage. I believe that pleased God. We wanted to honor Him, even though we both came from broken pasts.

Our children all got along great, and we treated them as if we were a married couple our whole adult lives. During our dating period, we were under relentless attack and persecution in many ways. Much of it was from certain family members who took it upon themselves to delve into my past. Without talking or meeting me, they attacked me and put me down as if I was an ex-convict. It was painful and hurtful, and brought back pains from my past. However, this time, we prayed together for help and healing, and we beat down the enemy's lies with the power of the Holy Spirit.

After much counseling, prayer, and preparation, we married one year later. The journey has been exactly what God had in mind. However, we have experienced ongoing attacks, none of which have derailed us in any way. We see the pathetic work of the enemy, and we are prayer warriors. These attacks have become worse from family. Family members have hurt our family with lies and attacks. Our adult children have been great, and we are in their lives as well as the lives of our grandchildren, helping them with prayer and raising the little ones, knowing that Jesus has saved them from eternal separation—*what a joy.*

To my brothers—The Lord promises to give us the desire of our hearts, as long as it does not go against His will. My wife and I have asked the Lord for forgiveness many times, and we have dedicated our marriage to Him.

Rick L.—What I have learned as a father over the years.

In considering the title of this section, the volume of things that God has taught me over the years became a bit daunting. When Fredrick asked if I would contribute an account of my mistakes as a father, I had no idea that I would be able to put it all inside a few pages. God is good. So, what I will share are the three things that I failed at the most; what I learned from those epic fails and how it impacted my children and my life. I pray that this helps you on your journey as a father.

What good is all the work I do if my kids do not get to know Jesus and become His disciples?

Probably one of the most important things that I learned as a dad is that God has no grandchildren. No matter what my relationship with God is, each of my children must make up their mind on whether to be a follower of Christ. My job is to be the ambassador for Christ to them so that they will have that chance.

This verse comes to mind. It is when Joshua confronts Israel with all that God has done for them and they need to make a choice.

> PROBABLY ONE OF THE MOST IMPORTANT THINGS THAT I LEARNED AS A DAD IS THAT GOD HAS NO GRANDCHILDREN. NO MATTER WHAT MY RELATIONSHIP WITH GOD IS, EACH OF MY CHILDREN MUST MAKE UP THEIR MIND ON WHETHER TO BE A FOLLOWER OF CHRIST. MY JOB IS TO BE THE AMBASSADOR FOR CHRIST TO THEM SO THAT THEY WILL HAVE THAT CHANCE.

Now therefore fear the Lord and serve him in sincerity and in faithfulness. Put away the gods that your fathers served beyond the River and in Egypt, and serve the Lord. And if it is evil in your eyes to serve the Lord, choose this day whom you will serve, whether the gods your fathers served in the region beyond the River, or the gods of the Amorites in whose land you dwell. But as for me and my house, we will serve the Lord. (Josh. 24:14–15 ESV)

The church in my home then becomes the most important church I serve (The Domestic Church, *Lumen Gentium*). My wife and children each need to experience the light of Christ in our household and see me living out my faith with my wife. This type of unity (John 17) allows them to believe that Jesus is the Christ. Everything else that comes along and all that I have learned beyond this fact is pure fluff in my life. Further, if I am not there as an ambassador to invest in my children, it will never happen.

As a young father, when I was twenty-three, life was just beginning. Married barely nine months before our first child was born, that was a time that I was just trying to keep my head above water. Just out of the US Navy, embarking on a career in computers and learning who I was, it was a time of heavy focus on myself. I needed to learn more to do my job so I could earn more to support my family. I needed to become a disciple and was still so very broken myself. I did not yet understand how important it was, doing this *with* my wife and not just for my wife. I was working lots of hours, away from home, in a job that had me traveling. My poor young wife was left at home to raise our kids, when she was in the same learning mode as I was.

So, this was a time when self-focus seemed important. The early years were more study for professional growth, with lots of hours at work, while trying to learn who I was in Christ. When you couple that with my nature of being very selfish, it was challenging for my wife and kids.

As I grew older, life seemed to be coming together. I started a business, had more involvement with church, more professional and personal study, and more hours away from home, all of which had a significant impact at home, and my wife felt alone. My time with my kids was good when I was there—*when I was there.*

Over time, God transformed me, taught me, and helped me understand my role as a father and husband—I cannot very well separate the two. That was a key learning point for me. My life as a father was completely tied to my life as a husband and as a disciple of Christ. My wife and I were to be one together, and we were meant to raise and teach our children together, not separately. As the family grew and matured, the kids all went their own way. The impact of my not being as active in their lives as I should have been was evident as they walked away from God. However, Proverbs 22:6 gives us hope. "Train the young in the way they should go; even when old, they will not swerve from it (ESV). Being faithful as the kids grew up would yield results as their lives unfolded.

It was good that I focused on the study of scriptures and becoming a disciple. It was good to be involved in the church. It would have been better if I had included my kids and wife, and not left them at home just because it was more convenient. When children see their parents actively serving God with them alongside, it makes a significant impact on them. Why? The impact is because as we are coming alongside them, we are making disciples. I was always ready to come alongside someone at church or in a small group to help them, but I usually did that at the expense of time with my children.

The domestic church, the church in my home, is the first and most important one I am called to. The one that follows is my broader family. It does not do any good if I am not bringing the Good News to my family and making disciples there but am out everywhere else doing that for others.

I am not saying that I am not to go out to all the world; I am saying that when Jesus said we would go to all the world, He started with the local place first, and the rest of the world came last. Bringing the world to Christ starts in my family. "But you will receive power when the Holy Spirit comes upon you, and you will be my witnesses in Jerusalem, throughout Judea and Samaria, and to the ends of the earth" (Acts 1:8 ESV).

Allow children to make mistakes; they learn best through failure. As a young man, patience was not my strong suit. To be brutally honest, it has been one of the biggest failings when my kids were young. I did not want to wait for them to learn, so I would step in and do it for them. Consequently, the human process of trial and error never kicked in to help them learn and become proficient at whatever they were doing. Correcting them in the middle of whatever they were doing also did not help inspire confidence in themselves. Instead, it caused second-guessing, quitting, and never getting beyond the first failure.

Fortunately, as I got older, I had some men in my life who taught me that valuable lesson, and I was able to teach my kids as well. It did not benefit my oldest sons as much as it did my daughter and youngest son, but over time and with the blessing of having a close relationship with my kids, I still can mentor them. Each has had some pretty epic failures, which we celebrate, on their way to success. I also have three stepdaughters with whom I have great relationships, that I have had the chance to impact and help. My learning to be patient with them and learning to let them fail and then helping them learn from their mistakes and failures have been a significant growth point in my own life as a dad.

Love them, whether they deserve it or not. I was pretty big on conditional love when I was young. Maybe not outwardly, but my actions certainly seemed that way. If you did the things I approved of, you got the nice dad. If you did things that I did not like, you got the grumpy dad.

It all started to come together at a retreat I was attending, and God was dealing with me about the kind of father I was. I cannot say it was the most comfortable, feel-good time I have ever had at a retreat, but it was the most fruitful. At one point, when I was being heavily convicted of my shortcomings as a father, and coming face-to-face with how amazing my Heavenly Father is, I prayed a prayer that I regretted uttering at some points in the journey but am thankful that God never let me off the hook for that prayer. I asked that God reveal His Father's heart to me so that I might become the kind of father that He wanted me to be to my children. Wow, did He answer that prayer! "We love because he first loved us" (1 John 4:19 ESV).

When I was a sailor, we had a saying when we were going into heavy seas that went something like this, "Now Stand By for heavy rolls; pitching fore and aft!" When we heard that, we knew it was going to get intense. The first time I heard that we were sailing in the North Atlantic in a hurricane. I remember having to tie myself into my rack (bed) by my wrist and opposite ankle just to get any rest. Well, after praying this prayer, that is exactly what happened in my life. There is also a saying that says, "Smooth seas never made a good sailor." I am here to tell you that God wanted me to be an excellent sailor!

Over the years, my children (I include my stepdaughters as they are my kids too) have, one by one, brought me to my knees in prayer and agony. But through it all, God was with me, showing me exactly how He loved me through the same types of things. He transformed my heart from a heart that put conditions on my love to a heart that simply loves my children. Then, He extended that to His children. What an incredible gift to receive from my Father in heaven—to replace my hard and selfish heart with one that loves because He first loved me.

Father God's love has redirected my focus in life from myself to others and started with my family. His love has helped me to be patient enough to allow my children to learn and to celebrate their most epic fails as steps along the way to success, and His love has taught me to love all of my children, all the way through, even when I don't like them.

Being a father is absolutely a journey, not a destination, and now that my kids are grown, our relationships have changed. Now I come alongside them with the Good News. Some of them I am helping to become disciples. All of them can see my Heavenly Father in me and how being one with my wife makes me a better dad, gramps, and man. They know that I am on a journey, and they all see how God can transform a selfish, impatient, unloving man into the opposite. They know that with God, all things are possible.

CHAPTER TEN

SALVATION

Therefore, if anyone is in Christ, the new creation has
come: The old has gone, the new is here!
—*2 Corinthians 5:17*

Rogers (Not his actual name) began the journey of his new creation by deciding to give his life to the Lord and accepting Him as his personal savior. His concern was the emptiness inside of him. His marriage had crumbled, which led to his addiction to drinking and smoking tobacco. When I met him, I knew deep down inside me he was empty in spirit and had found comfort in his drinking and smoking habits. While I sat reflecting and imagining how terrible life can be without Jesus, I became so restless. I just had to go talk with him.

I must confess that I struggled initially because I did not know how he would receive my message, or how and where to start the conversation. I approached him and before I knew it, our conversation started flowing. He poured his heart out and confirmed my thoughts about him. To him, nothing seemed to work. He had lost his job, and his marriage was in shambles. I could relate to his story, which led to my sharing what knowing Jesus could do in his life. He listened with interest, and by the time I finished, he accepted, surrendering his life to Jesus. I led him to Christ and prayed for him.

Becoming the head of the family starts with a man surrendering his life to Jesus. Without Him, we can do nothing. Every soul needs a comforter and when there is no comforter, most men gravitate toward womanizing,

> BECOMING THE HEAD OF THE FAMILY STARTS WITH A MAN SURRENDERING HIS LIFE TO JESUS. WITHOUT HIM, WE CAN DO NOTHING.

drinking, smoking, or doing drugs. This was exactly where Rogers found himself, but I thank God that he surrendered his life to Jesus.

The mistakes that men make most often happen during their life without Jesus. Families struggle and suffer when the head is without Jesus. There is a certain limit to how far a man can go with-

> THE MISTAKES THAT MEN MAKE MOST OFTEN HAPPEN DURING THEIR LIFE WITHOUT JESUS.

out Jesus, but with Him, there is no limit. Once Jesus comes into our life, we are able, through Him, to correct our past mistakes and change our behavior.

If you are reading this book and you have not yet given your life to Jesus Christ, I encourage you to do so. We cannot do it alone, but He can come into our lives and help us when we invite Him.

Working Out Your Salvation

> *Therefore, my dear friends, as you have always obeyed—not only in my presence, but now much more in my absence—continue to work out your salvation with fear and trembling, for it is God who works in you to will and to act in order to fulfill his good purpose.* (Phil. 2:12–13)

It is one thing to surrender your life to Christ, and it is a different thing to work out your salvation. I never completely understood this scripture before I got married. My life up to that time was not without Christ. Although I saw myself as holy and devoted, once married, I realized how ungodly I was inside my home. If there is a place to measure our growth in our salvation journey, it is in our own homes.

Again, I keep telling people that they do not really know who I am until they ask my wife or my children about me.

I KEEP TELLING PEOPLE THAT THEY DO NOT REALLY KNOW WHO I AM UNTIL THEY ASK MY WIFE OR MY CHILDREN ABOUT ME.

> *In the year that King Uzziah died, I saw the Lord, high and exalted, seated on a throne; and the train of his robe filled the temple. Above him were seraphim, each with six wings: With two wings they covered their faces, with two they covered their feet, and with two they were flying. And they were calling to one another: "Holy, holy, holy is the LORD Almighty; the whole earth is full of his glory." At the sound of their voices the doorposts and thresholds shook and the temple was filled with smoke. "Woe to me!" I cried. "I am ruined! For I am a man of unclean lips, and I live among a people of unclean lips, and my eyes have seen the King, the LORD Almighty." (Isa. 6:1–5)*

King Uzziah was not only a great king; he was highly favored by God. The circumstances that led to his death shook Isaiah, causing him to reflect on his life and realize how unclean he was. For me, when my marriage was heading toward divorce, my eyes were opened, and I saw how unclean I was.

Marriage is a good yardstick for measuring the maturity in our salvation. It is not just a matter of confessing the word of God or preaching to others. If men keep this instruction in their hearts, they will stay focused on working out their salvation daily. When we do this, it shapes the lives of our spouses and children positively. Practicing a righteous life at home makes us the role model. If my wife or children can testify that I am the man who influences positively, that is more than enough. Guess what—when my family is influenced positively because of how I live my life at home, the more interest they will have in living the same kind of life and the more love they will have for God.

Many children today have gone astray, not because they were not trained in Christian homes, but because they never saw Jesus in the lives of their dads. Children learn more from what they see than from what they have been taught. When a man abuses his wife regularly, either verbally or physically, their children are watching. They do not care how mighty you might be as a prayer warrior or how many times you do your devotions. What matters is how you are reflecting Jesus in your home.

Every head of the family should reflect on their life, identify what they are missing, and start working out their salvation. It is a daily exercise. No man on this planet earth can boast of arriving at perfection. We fail daily but the most important thing is to have a willing heart in working out our salvation.

Foundation

When the foundations are being destroyed, what can the righteous do? (Ps. 11:3)

Many men are struggling in their marriages because of a faulty foundation. When a man grows up observing his father abusing his mother, there is a tendency that he will repeat his father's behavior when he marries. Most times, dads who drink excessively will influence their children to do the same. I can go on and on listing examples; however, my point here remains that most of the things we see going wrong are because of the generational factor. When you acknowledge that, it becomes easier for the Holy Spirit to help.

For I know my transgressions, and my sin is always before me. (Ps. 51:3)

I grew up with anger and scolding in our home—and guess what? I found myself doing the same to my wife and children. In acknowledging this, I experienced instant deliverance. I see many people denying this fact, and so they struggle. I recognized my transgressions; what about you? Study your family foundation, acknowledge what has to be corrected, and seek the Holy Spirit to work through it with you. It is very amazing how, when we visit medical doctors, they want to know our family history. Many of the illnesses diagnosed are hereditary, and yet many men remain ignorant and continue to struggle. A helper is available through Jesus Christ.

Curse

Do not be deceived: God cannot be mocked. A man reaps what he sows. (Gal. 6:7)

Most of our struggles result from our past lives. That is why I started this chapter by explaining the importance of salvation. Many of us do not have a good testimony for our past. We have sowed our lives with harmful seed, and we reap what we sow. Thank God for the finished work of our Lord Jesus Christ at Calvary. He redeems us from the curses attached to our past lives if we surrender to Him. Those in Him are new creations and, behold, old things are passed away. When we come to Christ, the blood washes away our sins, and the consequences that follow those past sins are wiped away.

How can I curse those whom God has not cursed? How can I denounce those whom the LORD *has not denounced?* (Num. 23:8)

We can trace most of our struggles back to our past lives. They can also be caused by curses pronounced upon a member or members in our lineage. We are living in a wicked world. Many times, we are ignorant of the devices of the devil who still exists today. Some people feel they have been wronged after a business transaction or a relationship ends badly. Rather than forgiving and moving forward, they go through occult spells and pronounce curses on the offender. I have witnessed the struggles men go through because of occult spells. Do not be naïve; these unfortunately exist. God has allowed me to experience occultism. From what I experienced, the victims are usually those who are the most naïve. However, there is a name that is above every name. At the mention of the name Jesus, every knee will bow, and all tongues will confess that Jesus Christ is Lord. We have a covering when we are in the Lord. As Balaam told Balak, no spell can affect your life when you are in the Lord. It is very vital for every head of the family that their top priority is to be in the Lord.

Guilt

Therefore, there is now no condemnation for those who are in Christ Jesus, because through Christ Jesus the law of the Spirit who gives life has set you free from the law of sin and death. For what the law was powerless to do because it was weakened by the flesh, God did by sending his own Son in the likeness of sinful flesh to be a sin offering. And so he condemned sin in the flesh, in order that the righteous requirement of the law might be fully met in us, who do not live according to the flesh but according to the Spirit. (Rom. 8:1–4)

I encourage you that there is no more condemnation once you give your life to Christ. Never allow the devil to threaten you with those negative lifestyles of the past. You are now a new creation in Christ, and your past sins have passed away. Regardless of errors made in the past, God has forgiven you, and God wants you to use your story to win others to Christ. So, whenever the thought of your past life creeps back in, remind the devil about your freedom. Your future matters more than your past.

Decision

The jailer called for lights, rushed in and fell trembling before Paul and Silas. He then brought them out and asked, "Sirs, what must I do to be saved?" They replied, "Believe in the Lord Jesus, and you will be saved—you and your household." (Acts 16:29–31)

Rogers, the man I mentioned earlier, after hearing all I had to say about the power of salvation, made an immediate decision to surrender his life to Christ.

Taking the bold step in believing in the Lord Jesus is all you need to be saved. And the sweet thing about it is that you will not be saved alone; it will lead your family to salvation through your example. After Rogers gave his life to Christ, he realized immediately that his sins were forgiven, and he understood that his immediate task was to start working out his salvation. He wants to become a better head of his family, and he wants to be a better role model. By His grace, Rogers will surely attain and fulfill his purpose.

CHAPTER ELEVEN

RECONCILIATION

All this is from God, who reconciled us to himself through Christ and gave us the ministry of reconciliation.
—*2 Corinthians 5:18*

Reading this book thus far should bring any man to the point of thinking about how to reconcile with their spouse and how to affect their children positively. It is about swallowing the natural pride in every man by humbling oneself and doing God's will.

My marriage, as I have openly shared in this book, was heading down the route to divorce. By humbling myself, I keyed into doing God's will. Every man can do the same, if they choose to do so. My friend's parents had been divorced for twenty years; neither of them remarried. Luckily, when the man sought reconciliation, they eventually got back together again. I do not intend to bombard you with examples of couples that divorced but later reunited, but I say that reconciliation is possible and remains the heart of God because God hates divorce.

Where it is not possible to reconcile, many people remarry. It is rarer for divorced people to remain single. However, this chapter focuses on reconciliation, so I will not discuss remarriage here.

Steps to Reconciliation
Fulfill Your Obligation

> *Wives, submit yourselves to your own husbands as you do to the Lord.*
> *For the husband is the head of the wife as Christ is the head of the church,*
> *his body, of which he is the Savior. Now as the church submits to Christ,*
> *so also wives should submit to their husbands in everything. Husbands,*
> *love your wives, just as Christ loved the church and gave himself up for*
> *her. (Eph. 5:22–25)*

Often, a man will concentrate on the above verse, feeling that they have a right that they can hold over their wife. The more a man fights for this right, the more he moves astray from fulfilling his obligation. The wisdom here is to focus on fulfilling your own obligation, which is to love your wife. So, regardless of whether the wife is submissive or disrespectful, focus on loving unconditionally. The foolishness in the eyes of men is wisdom in the eyes of God. Men who stay focused on fulfilling their obligation will gain more respect and submissiveness than they yearn for from their wives. I noticed my wife spontaneously became more submissive and respectful the moment I took the first step to reconciliation and started fulfilling my obligation, as quoted in the verse above.

Taking Action

> *Do not merely listen to the word, and so deceive yourselves. Do what it*
> *says. Anyone who listens to the word but does not do what it says is like*
> *someone who looks at his face in a mirror and, after looking at himself,*
> *goes away and immediately forgets what he looks like. But whoever looks*
> *intently into the perfect law that gives freedom, and continues in it—not*
> *forgetting what they have heard, but doing it—they will be blessed in*
> *what they do. (James 1:22–25)*

Immediately get into action by applying all you have learned from this book. There is a wealth of knowledge in this book that can help you work towards reconciliation. Do not just read this book, thinking of it as powerful advice, and yet be unwilling to change your ways. Do not dismiss the book and not recognize the points that will cause or move you to make a positive difference or change. Note the chapters that affected you the most and begin taking steps toward putting the knowledge you gained into practice. Forgive your spouse, even when you know that you are right. Be the first to seek and begin reconciliation after any misunderstanding. Have patience with your family and listen to them. I struggled with this myself. I will next share a story about using the power of listening as a great means of reconciliation.

Power of Listening

My dear brothers and sisters, take note of this: Everyone should be quick to listen, slow to speak and slow to become angry, because human anger does not produce the righteousness that God desires. (James 1:19–20)

Kent married Stacy (actual names withheld) and eventually, they were blessed with two beautiful daughters. During a period of turmoil in the marriage, they separated. During the period of separation, while waiting for the last orders for their divorce, something strange happened. Kent started reflecting on the issues standing between him and Stacy. As he thought about it, he could not pick out exactly what he felt Stacy had done wrong. The more he thought about it, the more he felt the urge to sit down with Stacy and listen to her. He called Stacy, asked if they could meet, and told her that he wanted to sit and just listen to what she had to say. At first, Stacy was suspicious but decided to call and ask her lawyer before agreeing. Acting on her lawyer's advice, she accepted the meeting. Kent did exactly what he had promised to do—he just sat and let Stacy pour out her heart. As Stacy talked, she paused often to see if Kent would interrupt like he normally would do, but Kent never did. Stacy, at that point, felt a change in Kent's behavior. When Stacy finished her outpour and was waiting to hear what Kent had to say, Kent burst into tears. He asked Stacy to forgive him and asked if she would give him a second chance. Stacy did not understand what had happened. Kent confessed that he had never listened to her before. He could not think of anything else that had gone

THERE IS POWER IN LISTENING.

wrong with their relationship other than that he never listened to Stacy. Throughout their marriage, Stacy had repeatedly lamented "Kent, you never listen to me." Stacy forgave Kent, and they were able to reconcile. There is power in listening. Most men are guilty of not intentionally listening to their wives.

Return to Your Children

He will turn the hearts of the parents to their children, and the hearts of the children to their parents; or else I will come and strike the land with total destruction." (Mal. 4:6)

If you are estranged or at odds with your children, take the bold step of offering reconciliation. For as long as it takes, please make the effort toward reconciliation. Never dwell in guilt or wallow in your past mistakes. We all have blown it with our children in one area or the other. It is most important that we do our best in reconciling with our children wherever they are. It is one thing for you to take the initiative to do so, yet it is the child's responsibility to accept the reconciliation. Remember, do your best by offering reconciliation and then depend on the Lord to touch the hearts of your children.

Strength Made Available

An angel from heaven appeared to him and strengthened him. (Luke 22:43)

While on his journey to Calvary, Christ became weak and lost the strength to continue. He rested and reflected on all that had been placed on Him, and then He prayed asking that God take the burden from Him and not allow what was to happen. As he prayed fervently, He asked that it would not be His will but the will of God that would be done. Christ knew that it is the will of God that matters. Immediately after Christ said this, an angel appeared to Him and strengthened him.

Jesus went out as usual to the Mount of Olives, and his disciples followed him. On reaching the place, he said to them, "Pray that you will not fall into temptation." He withdrew about a stone's throw beyond them, knelt down and prayed, "Father, if you are willing, take this cup from me; yet not my will, but yours be done. (Luke 22:39–42)

For us to attain reconciliation, we first must acknowledge that reconciliation is the will of God. As you read, it might be difficult for you to completely understand what I am teaching in this section. I know this because it was hard for me too. Commit to doing God's will and pray the sincere prayer that Jesus prayed, asking God to let not your will but His will be done. I promise you, there is always strength made available when we choose to do God's will.

It was not an easy decision for Kent, but he took the first step to reconcile, and the necessary strength was made available. I have not told all the stories behind his struggles, but I want to let you know that it was a very tough journey. Saying that you are sorry to your wife or child is often difficult for men to do; however, remember it is not to be your will but God's will.

Patience

Be completely humble and gentle; be patient, bearing with one another in love. (Eph. 4:2)

I may repeat myself with this section heading, but I could not find a better word to replace patience as one step in reconciling. People need sufficient time to move past their hurts and heal. Unlike Stacy, who instantly forgave Kent and agreed to reconcile immediately, it may not be so easy for many people. Playing your part in initiating reconciliation should be your role, but your spouse or child agreeing and accepting is totally up to God. Humble yourself, be prayerful, and patiently wait until God touches their heart. I was privileged to be with a couple that was experiencing a shaky marriage. It got so bad that even the daughter was advising her mother to seek a divorce. I witnessed this young lady talking to her father rudely. I decided to talk with her about it. Later, I did so in the presence of her mother and truthfully brought up the consequences of her actions. She listened and agreed with all I had said. I asked her to apologize to her father, and before I left, she promised that she would. After a few weeks, I called the father to follow up and learned that he had never received an apology from his daughter. I then called the mother who explained things in detail to me. She said the daughter accepted my council and fully intended to apologize to her father, but she wanted the wound to heal first. Please understand that sometimes people will defer reconciliation. If your situation is taking a longer time than you expected, hang in there, and believe that God will touch every heart. Reconciliation is God's priority.

CHAPTER 12
CONCLUSION

At least there is hope for a tree:
If it is cut down, it will sprout again,
and its new shoots will not fail.
—*Job 14:7*

The best way to bring this book to a conclusion is to instill in all men the truth that hope is real. If you are having difficulties in your family relationships, have hope that your situation will change for good. Regardless of what the issues are, reflect on all you have read and renew your hope that they will be successfully resolved. Everything you have read in this book, including the contributed stories, can be used to reinforce your hope. Any conflict in your family, no matter how dire, can be amicably resolved.

With God, all things are possible to them that believe. Jesus Christ is the author and finisher. He alone is the one who can change the heart of your wife or your children. You cannot do it alone. Jesus has sent the Holy Spirit as a helper to those who believe. No man can change the heart of the wife or children, only the Holy Spirit. I encourage you to yield to the Lord and have Him fight for you. He is the one that will win the battle for you.

If you are thinking of leaving your marriage, please hang in there. I believe that in any marriage, depending on how God desires, there is no retreat and no surrender. The exception would be where life is threatened or in danger. Have hope that your honeymoon will bounce back again. Remember that there is a part for you to play. There is only one person you can change, and it is you. Practice all you have read in this book and watch the Lord play His part. Believe me, it is doable once you are determined to change your perspective and allow God total control over your life.

You have made mistakes in the past. Rest assured you are not alone. Everyone has made mistakes, and we will continue to do so. All have sinned and fallen short, so regardless of where you are, the most important thing is your genuine repentance and a willing heart to work out your salvation so you can be whom God expects you to be. God will surely take your mess and turn it around to be a message for others to learn from. The grace of God suffices to meet us in any circumstance we find ourselves in.

Have you become addicted to alcohol and drugs? There is always a second chance. Our God is a God of second chances. Confess and repent of your sins, and you will see your life revive. Are you in an adulterous situation? If so, your life can never be at peace. Run for your life if you are in an adulterous relationship with another woman. The devil has deceived many men to seek comfort by having a mistress. That is evil, and it is the very reason you have not received the comfort you seek. Recently, I heard troubling news of a married man who died in a hotel while with his mistress. Men, this is not how it should be. We all will die one day, but my prayer is for none of us to die shamefully. The legacy we leave behind is of great importance.

For those of you whose children have abandoned you, have hope and keep praying, believing that God will surely return them to you. Once you have retraced your errors and you are working out your salvation, God will surely help you. We discussed reconciliation in the previous chapter, and I encourage you to return to it often to help keep your hope alive.

In Summary

Now all has been heard; here is the conclusion of the matter: Fear God and keep his commandments, for this is the duty of all mankind. For

God will bring every deed into judgment, including every hidden thing, whether it is good or evil. (Eccles. 12:13–14)

I wrote this book for and about men, but it is not meant to be a condemnation of men. I know that they are not the sole cause of strife in their homes. Our focus has been on men because we are the head of the family, and as the head, we are the leaders. Every skilled leader makes sacrifices for his followers, in this case, his family. Therefore, if there should be any sacrifice made for a home to work, it should be by the man. This is not just an opinion; it is the truth. God's design is for the men to be the head of the family.

> OUR FOCUS HAS BEEN ON MEN BECAUSE WE ARE THE HEAD OF THE FAMILY, AND AS THE HEAD, WE ARE THE LEADERS. EVERY SKILLED LEADER MAKES SACRIFICES FOR HIS FOLLOWERS, IN THIS CASE, HIS FAMILY. THEREFORE, IF THERE SHOULD BE ANY SACRIFICE MADE FOR A HOME TO WORK, IT SHOULD BE BY THE MAN. THIS IS NOT JUST AN OPINION; IT IS THE TRUTH. GOD'S DESIGN IS FOR THE MEN TO BE THE HEAD OF THE FAMILY.

We cannot have a balanced home without the head of the family. You are the head of your family. Stand up, embrace your responsibilities, and encourage as many other men as possible to do the same. Become a man of influence and model your marriage for the younger generations to emulate and pass on to their sons. The original intention of God's institute of marriage must be restored in our society today. My dream is to have each head of the family fulfill their obligation by loving their wives and children unconditionally. When the family is perfectly balanced, our community will be balanced and likewise the state and nation.

> WHEN THE FAMILY IS PERFECTLY BALANCED, OUR COMMUNITY WILL BE BALANCED AND LIKEWISE THE STATE AND NATION.

This book results from what God has placed on my heart and in my hands. I have openly shared my testimony about my marriage and family. I have tried to relate and pour out all that has been laid on my heart. Although I do not know your present situation or predicament, I understand the frustration and stress you may be enduring.

The most important thing right now is that we work collectively to reduce the growing number of homes with absent fathers. May you be among the men who work hard to bring about the reduction of the absence of fathers at home. My dream is to have these statistics reduced drastically and I assure you I have hope and believe it will surely come to pass.

Return to this book often and reread the portions that apply to what you are experiencing at that moment. You will be strengthened and look at your challenges with a fresh view. When you have finished reading this book, close it, and determine to change those habits that have been causing conflict. Put all you have learned into immediate action. Remember to practice patience and do not expect instant results.

Stop condemning yourself and living in endless guilt. The devil is a liar. Pull down those negative thoughts; fight them daily through prayers and the word of God. Confess and repent of your evil ways. Who the Lord sets free is free indeed. That which lies ahead of you is what matters today and not the past. If God forgives you, no one can hold you back. Keep doing good, be available to serve your family, and let your love bloom and grow at home. Ask your family how you may help them. Listen more than you speak, and when you do speak, let the words that come out of your mouth be edifying and not harmful. Use your position as the head to encourage and support your family.

Invitation

Join those of us who have shared our story to affect other men so we can collectively reduce the number of homes without the head, those with absent fathers. I encourage you to write out your own story or testimony and share it with other men who are willing to be mentored. By being open and honest about your own experiences, you may positively affect another man to return to being the head of his family. The effect of this will be generational and not only save families but also lives.

I also advise you to find stories that relate to your life and situation. Explore how God turned those stories into meaningful testimonies. Hearing another person's testimony helps us keep our hope alive. If God did it for others, surely, He will do it for you.

I hope that you have gained insight and wisdom through the words I have written in this book. I felt the Holy Spirit fill me with the mission to write about the terrible effects a missing head has on a family. Before, during, and after writing the manuscript, I have sought the Lord's blessings and asked that His will would be transferred and reflected in what I wrote.

Please do not keep the message this book holds to yourself. Share it with family, friends, and those men you seek to mentor. I would love to hear your testimony of how you put the principles and actions I have outlined in this book in place to regain your role as the head. Although I have not met you yet, I pray for your continuing success!

In His Service,
Fredrick

REVIEWS

Not without the Head

"Mr. Ezeji-Okoye! Who are you? Why should I stand at your door and knock?" Those could have been the words of Jesus, asking the author if he was ready to take up his cross and follow Him. Were these the words our Lord and Savior spoken to Mr. Ezeji-Okoye? Were these words spoken years ago when a well-meaning and somewhat misguided man stood before his wife and children and wondered why life was not working out according to his plan? I don't know, but the words of his book are filled with the warmth of Jesus's love, and it is apparent that He is now walking hand in hand with the author through the challenges of marriage and fatherhood. The author's experiences and love come alive through his description of the impact of Christ's love on him and his family. Truly, the Ezeji-Okoye family is evidence of Divine Love.

Did Brother Fred hear the call of our Savior? Yes! His words convey the love, compassion, and correction of our Savior. Kneeling before Jesus, he has laid out his heart and soul in front of our Lord and shared with us his story of initially falling short of God's expectations, gaining humility as his awareness of God's love grew, and ultimately his redemption through God's love and forgiveness.

Did Brother Fred hear the call of our Savior? Yes! He did. He has followed the Savior's direction ever since: "Then said Jesus unto his disciples,

If any man will come after me, let him deny himself, and take up his cross, and follow me" (Matt. 16:24 KJV)."The author has recognized it is the work of a lifetime when we follow in the footsteps of our Lord.

This book is a valuable read for anyone who is working out his salvation, as Fredrick has, through marriage and fatherhood. It is a valuable read both for those of us that are already far along on the path and benefit from the wisdom of his experiences and for the man considering the journey.

The main themes of the book resonate strongly when viewed in today's society, which is seeing itself drift away from Christianity into secularism. Today, we are seeing Bible burnings in America on the news, something not seen since Nazi Germany. There are threats, *in America*, to tear down the crosses of Christian churches. The themes are: Dads—Get involved! You are a critical influence in your child's life. Your children will never be the same without you. Bring God into the picture. Listen to Jesus's knock and open the door! Dad, you are a difference-maker in the home! In today's world, you're absent too often. "His (my dad's) presence made an immense difference in my decisions," says Mr. Ezeji-Okoye.

God is missing from many twenty-first-century homes. And even where God is present, "many children grow up and walk away from God because the God we showed them at home makes little sense to them," laments the author. A sad statement of our human failings.

To bring the living God actively into our lives requires humility and hard work. Paul tells us in Philippians 2:12 (KJV) that we need to "work out our own salvation with fear and trembling." Is it easy to make sense to kids that God is central to their lives? The author says, "[No.] It is one thing to surrender your life to Christ and yet it is a different thing to work out of your salvation." A key part of working out the author's salvation has been to impart the fear of God to his children and help them nurture their faith.

But God hath chosen the foolish things of the world to confound the wise; and God hath chosen the weak things of the world to confound the things which are mighty. (1 Cor. 1:27 KJV)

How many of us have foolishly thought we were wise and strong? Isaiah told us to make the highway straight before the Lord, but too often we wander. How many of us have wasted so much time and energy because we thought we could do it our way instead of God's way? "Move over Lord; I've got this one." That's what our pride tells us. Mr. Ezeji-Okoye admits early in his marriage that he "...kept focusing on my wife's weaknesses without realizing her strengths." He and his wife are now partners in a growing relationship, with him as the head of the household.

> *Wherefore seeing we also are compassed about with so great a cloud of witnesses, let us lay aside every weight, and the sin which doth so easily beset us, and let us run with patience the race that is set before us....* (Heb. 12:1 KJV)

In twelve chapters, Brother Fredrick opens his Christian life before us with its failings, its shortcomings, and ultimately, his overcoming through opening that door to the Lord and asking Jesus into his life. When Jesus washes us in his blood, it is electric! Our Lord Jesus Christ has touched Mr. Ezeji-Okoye, and His guidance is alive throughout this book, in both the author's life experiences and how he shares those experiences with us, the readers.

The author starts by noting that everyone is different. Jesus told us in John 14:2 (KJV), "In my Father's house are many mansions." Yes, Lord, but I don't want everybody running off to their own mansion in my house! In marriage and relationships, our partners often don't match our preconceived notions and our initial expectations, and that is a good thing! The author instructs us that we need to be open to taking correction, whether it be from marriage counselors, pastors, mentors, or others.

The core of the book is a practical guide and roadmap of the tools our Savior has given to the author to help in his journey. For example, in Chapter 3, the author lays out specific steps for men to follow: "Work, manage, instruction, and completion."

These are basic building blocks for a husband and a father. He builds on these steps in the subsection entitled, "Man of Vision." The practical steps are:

- Build a personal altar
- Read the right books
- Create time to meditate
- Develop self-discipline
- Create a vision—from the words God has spoken to us
- Be transparent
- Manage your finances

The thread running through these seven key steps is the Bible, the living word of God!

It's the same thread that runs through the book as a whole.

This is a book I have read and will reread. I highly recommend it to newlyweds, new fathers, and those of us who are well along on the path of marriage. It is alive with the guidance and practical application of biblical principles. Its message resonates with all of us, no matter what our level of faith. Mr. Ezeji-Okoye has been guided by the Lord's Spirit to pray and share with us the experiences and lessons of his Christian journey.

James E Green
Assistant Pastor
Christian Fellowship Church
Richton Park, IL

***

I thoroughly enjoyed reading the pages of *Not without the Head*! The layout and flow of the text make it very easy to follow along, especially for men who are not avid readers, making the information accessible to a larger audience.

Fred presents realistic issues through his personal experiences and offers realistic solutions to readers. His writing is intended to draw attention to the various roles we play as well as the relatable nuances the average man experiences. Fred shares piercing truths for us men, for believers and non-believers both!

Not without the Head displays Fred as a transparent brother and leader as he presents practical and truthful painful points common among most men. This book provides options and answers that men can implement successfully. Additionally, Fred offers a subtle but honest rebuke that cuts sharply but heals gracefully through natural and spiritual application.

Chapter 6, "The Role Model" is one of my favorites. Fred does a great job presenting a model for mentoring, right in the pages of the book! A quote from the book that I will hold true to as a man, husband, father, and leader is, "Vision comes when a man draws close to his Creator and receives instruction. Faithfulness starts when a man becomes obedient to the word of God. A faithful head of the family is, therefore, that man, who after receiving instructions from God, becomes obedient to those instructions from God." Great work, my brother!

Anthony Thomas, Pastor
Calvary Covenant Church
Chicago, IL

***

Not without the Head is a comprehensive book on headship that guides husbands and fathers in accordance with the word of God. It carefully explains the mandate of the husband as the head of the home, emphasizing the essence of work and the helpmate given to him by God. It further explores the importance of husband and wife becoming one as ordained by God, the divine truth that serves as the bedrock for true fatherhood.

The book also explains the challenges experienced in marriage, with examples from the author's life experiences and those of others, and provides practical solutions to these challenges. This book addresses fatherhood, its essence, and how it can be made right amidst worldly challenges.

As a wife, mother, and pastor for over twenty-five years, this book is one of the best Christian works of literature that address the subject of headship. The content is in-depth, practicable, and above all, spirit-filled. The language is simple and accessible to everyone. Without mincing words, I believe that the writing and publication of the book is timely, especially in our present times where the headship of men as husbands and fathers is eroding from most homes, even in Christian homes. I highly recommend this book to every single young man before entering into marriage. To married folks, this book is the reviving catalyst you need to spice up your married life.

To Brother Fred, as we affectionately call the author, what an amazing book! God richly blessed you.

Dr. Cynthia Paintsil, MBA, MPH, DrPH.

***

Not without the Head is a masterpiece that explores the depth of the male dynamic, opening our eyes to real-life relatable scenarios where challenges can be changed to wins, whilst illustrating the importance of the male figure. This *life guide* is also supported by biblical references emphasizing the winning results that are guaranteed.

Sheila Oshuntuyi
Business Transformation Leader - HCSC
Founder: Suit Herself - Career Coaching Consultancy

***

Pastor Fredrick K. Ezeji-Okoye is addressing a big problem in our generation. I believe this book will help us and cause us to engage in the conversation on how we can begin to turn the table to establishing the sacred institution that God Himself ordained and commanded us to follow. *Not without the Head* is a book that is inspired to bring to order the things that Satan had been able to disrupt, disassemble, and in some cases, even destroy. This book will challenge the reader in many areas, not for condemnation, but for reconciliation and restoration of relationships with God the Father, and with their wives and children. It will cause us to bring to light things that are causing separation within the family, sometimes even unknowingly. Along with statistical references and personal past experiences Bro. Fred wisely added past experiences of other men who struggled from their own upbringing and how it affected their future relationships and marriages. I believe that the absence of the father in our society is the cause of many problems we face in our community today. In some cases, these problems or habitual practices have been handed down from generation to generation. This book can start the process of breaking generational curses and start a healing process that our nation desperately needs. We can turn the table and establish what God had originally intended.

Apostle David Cruz

***

ABOUT THE AUTHOR

Fredrick K. Ezeji-Okoye is the author of *Who Prays for the Pastor.*
He is a communicator at heart with a passion to share the Gospel both
orally and in writing. Among his many gifts and talents, he is a minister, writer, and motivational speaker with a mandate to equip and
empower the body of Christ by igniting a greater thirst and hunger for
God's word and intercessory prayer.

He is the founder and president of "The Men of Faith Network," a
fast-growing, diverse, and multicultural network of pastors and leaders
with global outreach. Fredrick is the CEO of The Liberty Foundation
LLC, a company that specializes in training church workers and con-
sultants. He lives in the Chicago metro area with his wife Ijeoma and
their three children, Chisom, Nkiruka, and Chinenye.

www.menoffaithnetwork.org
https://libertyfoundationllc.com/